KING SAUL,
THE TRAGIC HERO

also by John A. Sanford
published by Paulist Press

MINISTRY BURNOUT
HEALING AND WHOLENESS
DREAMS AND HEALING
THE INVISIBLE PARTNERS
THE KINGDOM WITHIN
THE MAN WHO WRESTLED WITH GOD
BETWEEN PEOPLE: COMMUNICATING ONE-TO-ONE
THE MAN WHO LOST HIS SHADOW
FRITZ KUNKEL: SELECTED WRITINGS

KING SAUL,
THE TRAGIC HERO

A Study in Individuation

John A. Sanford

PAULIST PRESS
New York/Mahwah

Library of Congress
Catalog Card Number: 84-61023

ISBN: 0-8091-2658-3

Published by Paulist Press
997 Macarthur Boulevard
Mahwah, N.J. 07430

Printed and bound in the
United States of America

Contents

Acknowledgments

My thanks to Helen Macey,
who as always helped me immensely
with the preparation of this manuscript,
and to Sherry Hartwell who,
in a letter many years ago,
in which she commented on lectures
I had given on Saul,
gave me an important clue to
an understanding of his story.

Dedication

To
James Kirsch

Introduction

It's the last of the ninth inning. The score is three to two in favor of the other side; your team has the bases loaded, there are two outs, and you're the batter. All eyes are on you as you walk out to the plate. Tension mounts as the opposing pitcher eyes you disdainfully. If you hit a home run, or even a solid single, you'll be a hero, and everyone will cheer as you round the bases, driving in the scoring runs ahead of you. When you get back to home plate your teammates will shake your hand and clap you on the back enthusiastically. Even the opposing pitcher will have to respect you now as he slinks back to the dugout, because that's what it means to be a hero.

This book is a psychological study of a man who could have been a hero like this, but didn't quite make it. At first glance it might seem as though I would have done better to study the life of a successful hero—a Washington or Queen Elizabeth I—someone who is remembered even today by a grateful people. But sometimes we learn more from a person who failed. In fact, the lives of those who are successful may make us who live ordinary lives feel so inferior that we let them be the heroes for us while we languish in our mediocrity.

Besides, there is more than one way to be a hero. Let's say you're the batter with the bases loaded and you don't hit a home run—you strike out. You won't be a hero then—at least you won't feel like one—and no one else will think you're one as you walk dejectedly to the dugout wishing you were invisible. Yet you might still be a hero deep inside if you were scared to death when you came up to the plate, and trembled when the pitcher fired his fast ball at you, but were determined to do your best and went down swinging.

Saul was a man who struck out, and it's easy to see why history remembers him as a failure instead of as a hero. One of the goals of this book is to learn from the difficulties of Saul's life certain things about that process of becoming a whole person that C.G. Jung called individuation. Saul's failures and mistakes may prove more instructive than the successes of others. We may even learn enough from Saul's tragedy to avoid a few unnecessary mistakes of our own.

In order to do this, however, we need to have the proper background in both biblical scholarship and psychology. For this reason I include a brief sketch of the historical situation in Israel at the time of Saul, and of the findings of biblical scholarship about the story. I also include in an appendix a brief synopsis of the psychology of C.G. Jung and Fritz Kunkel. It may be that most people who read this book will have read enough of my earlier books or other psychological material so that they are already familiar with these two psychologists. If you are one of these people, you will not need to read this appendix and will prefer to go directly to the biblical scholarship material and on to Chapter One, which begins our analysis of Saul.

I have said that Saul was a man who struck out. And strike out he did, but sometimes we get several tries at the plate. There is a question about Saul: tragic failure though he was, is it possible that at the very end he was a hero after all? Not the kind who hits a home run with the bases loaded while everybody is watching, but someone who acts heroically even when his cause is hopeless and nobody is watching? This is the question that you, the reader, will have to decide for yourself when you reach the end of this book.

Biblical Scholarship
Looks at Our Story

The story of Saul is found in what we now know as the First Book of Samuel, but originally 1 and 2 Samuel were parts of a longer work, the Deuteronomic History which included Deuteronomy, Joshua, Judges, the Books of Samuel and 1 and 2 Kings. It was only when the Hebrew Old Testament was translated into Greek in the third century B.C. that the books now known as 1 and 2 Samuel were created as separate documents. This point is of more than passing interest because in the Second Book of Samuel the central character is David. The fact that at one time 1 and 2 Samuel were part of one document suggests that originally the story of Saul and the story of David were regarded as one story, not two. As we will see, David plays an important role in Saul's life, and from time to time we will turn the spotlight from Saul to David in order to learn from the contrast between the two men.

Together with the stories of Jacob, Joseph, and Moses, the stories about Saul are from the oldest strata of the Old Testament. They are so old that originally they were told rather than written. This is important because it is the storyteller's art to tell as much as is necessary but nothing that isn't necessary. As a result, tales told by a storyteller have a dynamic power and immediacy that can't be found in the more embellished style of those who write.

No one has identified the original raconteurs who preserved the story of Saul, but we have reason to believe that these storytellers came from two different traditions because so many parts of the story are told in two, or sometimes even three, different versions. For instance there are two versions of how Saul tried to kill David, of Saul's first "sin," of how David spared Saul's life, and three versions of how David first came to Saul's court.

Sometimes these different versions of the same event only differ in details, but sometimes they vary from each other considerably. Scholars account for this with the hypothesis that some of the stories came from people who wanted a king over Israel and some from people who didn't. The first group of stories is called the Royalist tradition, and the second the Anti-Royalist tradition.

If I were a biblical scholar I would go into considerable detail about the different traditions and explain why versions of the same event differ from each other. However, I am not writing as a biblical scholar but as a person interested in the cure of souls. For this reason, when we come to a part of the narrative that has two or more versions from which to choose I will arbitrarily select the version that is the most psychologically instructive. In order not to interrupt the flow of the narrative I will not stop to defend my choice or even point out the existence of a separate version, except in the case of Saul's purported disobedience to Yahweh. In this instance there is an appendix in which I explain and defend why I chose one version and rejected the other.

If there are conflicting versions of the same incident the question naturally arises whether any of the accounts are historically trustworthy. If the tales were preserved and handed down throughout the centuries by various raconteurs, each of whom had a particular bias, the historical reliability of the Saul and David saga is even more questionable. The issue of historical reliability is one which justifiably concerns the biblical scholars, who are quite divided on the issue, some doubting the reliability of any of the stories, and others asserting that a true history can be found in them. However, since this book is concerned with a psychological analysis of the major character in the saga—Saul—it is not of great importance whether we are dealing with history or a mixture of history and imagination. In either case, a distinct personality emerges in the tales, who, much in the manner of Shakespeare's Hamlet, is a proper subject for psychological scrutiny and analysis. My personal preference is to believe that we have in the First Book of Samuel a basically reliable historical account, but if tomorrow I should learn that a character named Saul never even existed it would not in any way detract from the psychological study that I have attempted. For in a true literary figure, as in actual life, the archetypes that guide human life and destiny emerge and can be fruitfully studied for our edification.

This is as good a place as any to make my confession. In the introduction I said that one of the goals of this book is to help us learn about individuation. The other goal is to defend Saul against the generally negative judgment of history. The truth is, I may not be entirely objective in the point of view I present in this book because I am not writing as a dispassionate scholar but more as an attorney for the defense.

When I was a boy, more years ago than I like to remember, I used to read Hurlbut's *Story of the Bible*, and I was fascinated by the story of King Saul. Even then it seemed to my boyish mind and spirit that in spite of his obvious shortcomings the man was getting a "bad press." Certainly my Sunday School teachers didn't think much of him. Samuel, on the other hand, I didn't care for even though his virtues were roundly extolled by a variety of teachers who urged us boys to pattern our lives after his (that is, to be obedient). Through all the years my feeling has not changed, and now at long last I feel moved and equipped to leap to the defense of the much

maligned Saul. But of course an attorney for the defense cannot be counted on for objectivity. He will certainly concentrate on those facts that are important for his case, and
downplay those facts that do not support the points he is
trying to make. The astute reader may be offended at my bias,
and this may especially be the case with my treatment of Samuel, who is the major witness, as it were, against Saul. Now an
attorney for the defense may try to discredit the credentials of
the key witness against his client and I realize that I am open to
this charge when it comes to my treatment of Samuel.

However, although an attorney for the defense may be
biased he does not ignore the truth. In fact, a good counselor
may be effective not because he obscures the facts but because
he is motivated to discover facts that others have overlooked.
So while I admit to my bias, I also claim that there are certain
facts and nuances to Saul's story that commentators and his-
torians have disregarded that are important for a proper eval-
uation of Saul's character and place in history. It is these facts
I intend to bring out as I defend a man who has generally been
denied his proper place in history. If these facts do little credit
to Samuel, that can't be helped.

Now that I have made my confession, let's return to the
historical background of our tale. Until the time of Saul there
had been no king in Israel except Yahweh, who alone was acknowledged as ruler over his people. Ancient Israel had virtually no political structure; in fact it can hardly be said to have
existed as a nation at all in the modern sense of the word. The
social structure was based on the family, then the clan, and
then the tribe. The twelve tribes were related by a common
history, language, and religion, but there was no central gov-
ernment, no political constitution, and no standing army.
When an emergency arose that affected all the tribes an *ad hoc*
leader might be chosen to deal with the problem. The Book of
Judges tells the story of the various "judges" who were given

temporary authority because of such emergencies, but once the crisis was over the leadership role of that person ended.

This political system would have satisfied the most rabid anti-governmentalist of our time, but it was bound to come to grief when Israel's enemies became more effective. This happened when the Philistines, a vigorous and warlike people who lived west of the Israelites on the coast of the Mediterranean, began to encroach on Israel's territory. In about the year 1050 B.C. the Philistines invaded Israel and defeated a hastily assembled Israelite army at the town of Aphek. With the help of Samuel, the Israelites managed to avoid being completely taken over by the Philistines, but they were still dominated by them, and lived in fear of their great military power.

When the story of Saul begins Israel is oppressed not only by the Philistines but by other enemies as well, especially warlike nomadic tribes like the Amalekites, who roamed the fringes of Israel's territory, raiding the people and occasionally besieging a whole city. Under this kind of pressure it was natural that many of the Hebrews began to want a king. They saw that other nations around them had kings, and supposed that if they had a single ruler over them he could organize a standing army and defend them against their enemies.

These ideas, however, were counter to the traditional religious spirit of Israel that said only Yahweh was king. The more religiously conservative element therefore opposed the idea of a monarchy and argued that it was disloyal to Yahweh to want a king. Never mind that Yahweh hadn't been all that much help lately in the struggle with the Philistines; if you were only faithful to him, he would surely come through eventually. Besides, Yahweh was known to be a jealous God; he might resent it if the Israelites asked for a king and take it as a sign that they had forgotten his goodness to them in days gone by.

This was the political situation that existed when Samuel

was an old man. Because Samuel is so important to our story
he needs some words of introduction. The first seven chapters
of 1 Samuel tell us most of his story. His mother, Hannah, was
barren, but she prayed fervently to Yahweh for a child. Yahweh granted her prayer and she gave birth to a son, whom she
named Samu-el, which means "Name of God." Grateful to
Yahweh, Hannah dedicated the boy Samuel to Yahweh, and
when he was old enough she sent him to live with the priest Eli
in the temple.   *"Heard of God"*

One day when the boy was resting after attending to the
half-blind old priest, he heard his name called—"Samuel!
Samuel!" Thinking it was Eli, he went to him, but Eli said, "I
did not call; go back and lie down." This happened three
times. After the third time Eli knew it was Yahweh calling. He
said to Samuel, "Go and lie down, and if someone calls say,
'Speak, Yahweh, your servant is listening' " (1 Samuel 3:1–9).

Thus began a special relationship between Samuel and
Yahweh. While we don't know much about Samuel's later life,
we do know that he purified the worship of Yahweh from for-
eign elements, inspired resistance against the Philistines, and
judged the people in their disputes, making an annual journey
through the land for that purpose. Because there was no political structure in Israel, Samuel held no political office, but his
natural abilities, towering personality, and reputation for a
"talking" relationship with Yahweh gave him great status
among the Israelites. As far as the people of Israel were concerned, Yahweh spoke to them through Samuel, and therefore
everything Samuel said carried great weight.

However, no one is perfect, not even Samuel, and there
were some chinks in his armor of righteousness that not even
his devoted followers could entirely ignore. As we will see,
these deficiencies in Samuel's character, and his unawareness
of them, will have a considerable influence on our story.

This was the situation at the time Saul was chosen to be

the first king of Israel. The date is about 1030 B.C., and Saul is destined to reign until about 1010 B.C., when, after a seven year civil war, he is succeeded by David who reigned until 970 B.C. How Saul was chosen to be the king and what happened after that is the subject of our tale, to which we will now turn.

1

The People Want a King

Tolstoy began his novel *Anna Karenina:* "All happy families resemble one another; each unhappy family is unhappy in its own fashion." Ancient Israel definitely was an unhappy family, and our story begins with an especially unhappy time in Israel's turbulent history. On all sides the enemies of the Israelites are threatening them, and Samuel, who is now an old man, has appointed his two dishonest sons to be judges in the land in his place. The situation is so bad that the people finally complain:

> When Samuel grew old, he appointed his two sons as judges over Israel. The name of the first-born was Joel, that of the younger Abijah; they were judges in Beersheba. But his sons did not follow his ways; they wanted money, taking bribes and perverting justice. Then all the elders of Israel gathered together and came to Samuel at Ramah. 'Look,' they said to him 'you are old, and your sons do not follow your ways. So give us a king to rule over us, like the other nations' (1 Samuel 8:1–6).

Samuel didn't like what the people told him so he brought the matter up with Yahweh:

> It displeased Samuel that they should say, 'Let us have a king to rule us,' so he prayed to Yahweh. But Yahweh said to Samuel, 'Obey the voice of the people in all that they say to you, for it is not you they have rejected; they have rejected me from ruling over them. All they have done to me from the day I brought them out of Egypt until now— they deserted me and served other gods—they are doing now to you. Well then, obey their voice; only, you must warn them solemnly and instruct them in the rights of the king who is to reign over them' (1 Samuel 8:7–9).

Samuel follows Yahweh's instructions and warns the people: a king will take their sons into his army; he will make them plow the land and harvest his crops and produce weapons of war, and even take their daughters into his service; he will take the best fruits of the field for his officials, and tax their crops and flocks, and demand so much from them that they will be like slaves to him. When that happens, Samuel says darkly, everyone will cry out and complain to God, but Yahweh will not answer them. But in spite of Samuel's gloomy warning the people continue to clamor for a king, so Samuel talks with Yahweh again, and Yahweh says to Samuel, "Obey their voice and give them a king." The people are then dismissed by Samuel and return to their homes.

It is interesting that the first reason the people want a king is not to have someone help them against their enemies but because of their complaint about Samuel's two sons. Samuel had appointed his sons as judges, but the people say they don't follow his ways; instead they take bribes and pervert justice. The situation is now at a critical stage because Samuel is an old man; when he dies the people will be stuck with his two sons.

Much the same thing happened with the old priest Eli; his

two sons, Hophni and Phinehas, were also evil men who used their sacred function as priests for their own benefit:

> Now the sons of Eli were scoundrels; they cared nothing for Yahweh nor for the rights of the priests as regards the people (1 Samuel 2:12).

Like Samuel, Eli also "came to hear of everything that his sons were doing to all Israel." The honest old priest was so upset that he went to his sons and said:

> "Why do you do these things I hear from all the people? No, my sons! The reports I hear are not good . . ." (1 Samuel 2:22–24).

Eli took the complaints about his sons seriously, even though it must have been distressing to him, and he went to his sons and tried to correct them. However, Samuel doesn't do anything. Not only doesn't he go to his sons and try to do something about them, he doesn't even acknowledge the complaints of the people. It's as though Samuel doesn't even hear what the people are saying; he completely ignores the fact that his sons are dishonest and the people have a right to be upset. It's surprising to find this allegation against Samuel's sons in this particular narrative because it comes from the Anti-Royalist tradition which generally exalts Samuel and denigrates Saul. It seems to have escaped the attention of just about everyone that this bit about Samuel's sons puts Samuel in a bad light.

It's hard on parents when things go wrong with their children. Modern psychology, from Sigmund Freud on, has argued that problems people have in adult life can be traced back to disturbances in childhood; "negative parenting" distorts the growing child's personality bringing about problems later in life. Most parents today are more or less aware of the findings of psychology in this regard, and feel defensive or guilty when their children become problems to themselves or others. Even in Samuel's day a parent must have felt embarrassed and somehow responsible for the behavior of his or her children. For instance, the knowledge that children are influenced by their parents is found in a saying quoted by the Bible in two places: "The fathers have eaten sour grapes, and the children's teeth are set on edge" (Ezekiel 18:2 and Jeremiah 31:29 KJV).

In fact, however, parental responsibility for the children is exaggerated. There is also society and its influences at work on the children. And the bottom line is that there are certain things no parent can give a child. No parent can take away from the child the necessity for the young person to undergo her own individuation. And no parent can give to the child the gift of psychological consciousness. This each person must acquire on his own. Even the best parents can't arrange their children's lives in such a way that they make no mistakes. In fact, mistakes *must* be made if growth is to take place. As analyst David Hart once put it, "The wrong way has to precede the right way."[1]

What this means for those of us who are parents is that when things go wrong for our children we mustn't play God, but we must *look* at the problem. If we shoulder all the blame for the situation, we have an inflated idea of our significance in the total scheme of things. Are we God, after all, responsible for the way things are in this world? On the other hand, we must examine the situation in order to become aware of our shadow, that is, of those areas of unconsciousness on our part that may have influenced our children destructively.

It takes quite a bit of inner balance to see our influence on

---

1. From an article entitled "The Path to Wholeness" in *Psychological Perspectives*, Fall, 1972, p. 154.

our children in both its good and bad light and still not fall into
self-rejection, and evidently Samuel didn't have it, so he just
refused to look at what the people were saying about his sons.
This tells us that Samuel was more interested in protecting
himself than he was in the truth. Of course it might be argued
that Samuel lacked the understanding of modern psychology
so had no incentive to look at what was happening with his
sons. However, Eli faced up to what his children were doing,
so why shouldn't Samuel? Elsewhere in the Bible we read that
Jacob took a good hard look at his arrogant teenager, Joseph,
and tried to correct him, and David certainly was aware of exactly how treacherous his son Absalom was. But Samuel pre-
fers to remain blind, and this shows a lack of self-reflection and
a high degree of defensiveness.

In a lesser person than Samuel such egocentricity might
hurt only a few people, or even prove to be nothing more than
an annoyance, but because of the stature of Samuel's personality his egocentricity has far-reaching consequences. For
Samuel isn't just egocentric; he also has a genuine relationship
with Yahweh, and from this emerges a powerful personality
that puts him in a position to do either great good or great evil.
Until now the evidence is that Samuel has been a generally
positive influence among the Israelites, who understandably
looked to him for guidance. But when he appointed his evil
sons to be judges things began to go wrong, and when he refused to listen to the complaints of the people they went from
bad to worse.

We see in Samuel an example of how people live from
both their Real Self and their egocentricity. Samuel's inner authority and leadership ability come from the Real Self, but his
personality is marred by an egocentricity that he refuses to
face. To be sure, Samuel espouses the highest possible system
of moral values, but unfortunately our system of moral values
operates only within the range of consciousness; whatever we

don't know about ourselves remains unaffected by our moral code. This is one reason why self-knowledge is so extremely important, especially for persons in high places whose lives and decisions influence others.

Another reason knowledge of oneself is important is because of the psychological mechanism known as "projection." Projection occurs when we see some part of ourselves we know little or nothing about in someone else. Projection is not something that we do consciously; it is an unconscious mechanism in which images from within ourselves are projected onto other people. It's like sitting in a movie theatre watching a film. Our attention is riveted on the screen in front of us where we see the images of the actors, but the actual source of these images lies in the projecting machine behind us. This is the way it is with psychological projection: We see aspects of ourselves in projection on other people who are like a screen to us, when the source lies behind us, that is, in the unconscious.

Projection distorts human relationships, and is especially destructive when our dark side, the shadow, is projected onto other people. In family life, for instance, parents can project their shadow onto one of their children. They then react punitively to that child, or, as suggested before, the child may be forced to live out the parents' shadow projection. In society members of one race frequently project their shadow onto members of another race with results that are sometimes profoundly evil; this is certainly what happened with the Nazis who projected their rejected and unrecognized inferior side onto the Jews. Projection can also influence international relationships. Since World War II the Russians and the Americans have projected their shadows onto each other, and this has created a hostile paranoia that threatens to destroy the world.

This is why psychology is not just something for people who are troubled and go to a psychotherapist for help; it is enormously important for all of us. Ignorance of ourselves has grievous social and political as well as personal implications. It's especially important that leaders of nations, or other persons in positions of influence, have a marked degree of psychological awareness.

Samuel is a case in point. Samuel did not face his shadow. Therefore he believed himself to be righteous, and projected his shadow onto others, specifically, as we shall see, onto Saul. This not only was more of a burden than Saul could bear; it also brought misfortune upon Israel precisely because Samuel was such an important person. Of course it never occurred to Samuel that there was anything wrong with *him*. He had the kind of self-righteousness that comes from an egocentric system that seems to be working. As far as Samuel was concerned he was the one and only true prophet of Yahweh. This self-deception is the reason Fritz Kunkel once wrote:

> The Ego without knowing it is always fighting on the side
> of evil and darkness, although it pretends to be a servant of
> light.[2]

When the people told Samuel about his sons he didn't listen, but he did have an emotional reaction: He took the criticisms of the people and their request for a king personally. This personalistic reaction is revealed in what Yahweh said to Samuel:

> 'Obey the voice of the people in all that they say to you,
> for it is not you they have rejected; they have rejected me
> from ruling over them' (1 Samuel 8:7).

Samuel felt rejected when the people asked for a king, and

---

2. *Fritz Kunkel: Selected Writings.* New York: Paulist Press, 1984, p. 387.

so did Yahweh—at least he did if we can accept what Samuel reported. We have to remember when we read one of Yahweh's speeches that no one knows what Yahweh said except Samuel, and Samuel's personalistic reaction and general unawareness of himself may well have colored his memory. If Samuel had faced his own emotions a lot of trouble could have been avoided. He might have said to himself, "Why am I feeling so hurt and rejected by all of this?" But if he was aware of his hurt feelings at all, the indications are that he quickly buried them.

This brings us to an important point about masculine psychology (and feminine psychology too as we will see later). When a man's feelings are hurt, it is important that he face them consciously and do something with them if he can. Usually it is best to bring the matter up with the person who has offended him. For instance, if a man's feelings have been hurt by his wife he might say, "What you said really made me angry . . ." or "When you made disparaging remarks about me at the party last night it really hurt my feelings." Then the feeling is out in the open, and there is the possibility it can be dealt with in a related way. Even if the difficulty isn't resolved, at least the feelings remain conscious and aren't just buried.

Of course it isn't always possible to bring things up in a relationship. For instance, if our boss has hurt our feelings we may decide we don't have that option. But it's still possible to deal with the injured feelings by keeping them conscious, writing them down in our journal, or talking over the situation with a trusted friend or confidant. The trouble is that if the injured feelings are ignored they don't vanish; they fall into the unconscious, and when a man's hurt feelings do that, the "anima" gets hold of them.

The anima is the name Jung gave to the feminine side of a man. A man is not completely masculine but has a strong feminine component as well. Since his ego identifies with his masculine nature his feminine nature lives like an inner woman in the unconscious. Like many a real woman, the anima has a keen sense of justice when it comes to matters of personal relationship. When the anima gets her hands on a feeling of personal injury she sees it as a matter that must be resolved. Seen through her eyes the matter is intensified and exaggerated, and although the man might like to forget the troublesome situation his anima isn't about to do so. The result is that the man becomes possessed by a dark, vindictive mood. Although he doesn't realize it, his inner woman now has him in her grip, and is plotting revenge on the offending person.

Imagine that you live in a house with a trapdoor that leads into a big basement. Someone hurts your feelings, and since it's all very unpleasant you decide to open the trapdoor and drop the hurt into the basement. This way you think you have gotten rid of it, but down in the basement is the woman part of you and when the hurt feeling falls through the trapdoor she gets hold of it and nurses it carefully until it grows and grows and gathers all kinds of affect around it. The anima then sends up a lot of emotion, which, like a fog, seeps through the trapdoor and engulfs you until you are in a poisonous mood. Naturally other people around you are affected by the mood which poisons them too. Furthermore, because of the unconscious sense of injustice, you have a self-righteous feeling that projects guilt onto everyone else. One day something else happens that hurts you or makes you angry and you open the trapdoor to drop this incident out of sight as you did the other incidents, but by now the basement is so full it won't hold anything else. Before you can shut the door a host of devils comes pouring out. You experience this as a violent emotional eruption. In psychology we refer to this as an "anima attack."

The more egocentric a man is the worse is his relationship with his feminine side. Such men are especially likely to be preyed upon by the anima in a negative way and to be subject to "witchlike" moods and affects. The anima, however, is not to blame. If a man would relate to people honestly and not egocentrically, he would deal with his personal feelings directly and consciously and the anima wouldn't have to do the reacting for him.

Much the same thing is true for a woman. If she tries to avoid dealing with her sense of personal injury and drops it into her basement, her masculine side, the "animus," picks it up and plots revenge. He waits by the trapdoor with his club, and one day when the opportunity presents itself out he comes and lets the offending person (or anyone else who gets in the way) have it with his club.[3]

Samuel needed to do something with his hurt feelings. He might have said to the people who complained about his sons, "You offended me when you accused my sons of being dishonest. After all I've done for you during these years all you can do is complain. It makes me feel as though you don't appreciate me. And now you say you want a king. It's as though I don't mean anything to you anymore."

If he had answered the people in this way the matter could have been talked over. The people would no doubt have reassured Samuel of their affection and respect for him and Samuel would have felt better. Even if they didn't, he would have openly stated what he felt and kept his feelings out in the open. The anima would then have been satisfied because the right thing had been done in the relationship with the people.

Since Samuel didn't do anything like this, but followed the "drop it into the basement" technique, his hurt feelings fell into the clutches of the anima, and for the remainder of our story Samuel is gripped by an anima-inspired vindictive

---

3. See my book *The Invisible Partners* for a more complete description of the way the anima and animus influence the psychology of men and women and affect the way men and women relate to each other.

mood. This vindictiveness is soon directed at Saul, for, as we will see, Saul was the one who was chosen to be the king and to replace Samuel as the leading person in Israel. Clearly our story of the first king of Israel is off to an ominous start.

2

A King Is Chosen

Confronted by the inevitable, Samuel proceeds to select the man who is to be the king:

> Samuel called the people together to Yahweh at Mizpah and said to the Israelites, 'Yahweh the God of Israel has spoken and says, "I brought Israel out of Egypt and delivered you from the power of the Egyptians and of all the kingdoms that were oppressing you." But today you have rejected your God, he who saved you from all your calamities and desperate straits; and you have said, "No, you must set a king over us." Well then, take your positions before Yahweh according to your tribes and clans' (1 Samuel 10:17–20).

It's not hard to detect the note of resentment in Samuel as he grudgingly goes about his work. As the spiritual leader Samuel might have made a positive and hopeful speech to raise the morale of the people—who needed it, oppressed as they were by the Philistines, not to mention Samuel's sons. But Samuel used the occasion to castigate the people for what he regards as their unfaithful attitude, and once again the word "rejection" comes out: "But today you have *rejected* your God. . . ."

We can't be sure how God felt about all this, but we can be sure that *Samuel* felt rejected. Moreover, when he accused the people of rejecting God he surely projected his own rejected feeling into them. They aren't rejecting Samuel; it's he who is rejecting them because of his hurt feelings. This is the way unrecognized feelings distort the leadership capacity of even great personalities such as Samuel. Small wonder Samuel concludes his gloomy speech with the command, "You have said, 'No, you must set a king over us.' Well then, take your position before Yahweh . . ." which implies that one day Samuel will be able to tell the people, "See, I told you so."

Samuel now goes about his work. He calls forward the tribes of Israel and then casts the sacred lots to determine which tribe the future king belongs to. The lot falls to the tribe of Benjamin. Then he calls forward each of the clans of the tribe of Benjamin and the lot falls to the clan of Matri. Then he calls forward each man from the clan of Matri and the lot falls to Saul.

This may seem to us like a strange way to choose a king, but it didn't seem so to the ancient Hebrews because they believed that Yahweh guided the lots as they fell. Every ancient people had its method of divination, that is, ascertaining the mind of God as it related to a particular situation. The Romans used to kill a bird and cut it open; the way the entrails were shaped gave them an answer from the gods to their questions. When the Navajos had an especially important matter to decide they sent four shamans to the "Shining Sands," at the junction of two rivers. "Where the rivers met, there was an expanse of bright sand thinly covered with slowly moving water. The message the gods had written for them through the night would be drawn in symbolic design in the sand under the water."[1] By reading the meaning in the shapes of the sands the shamans could ascertain the will of the gods for their people. The ancient Chinese had the most sophisticated method of all: the *I Ching*, or Book of Changes. This profound book enables a person, through meditation upon a hexagram full of symbolic meaning, to relate to Tao, the Will of Heaven, and therefore act correctly with regard to any given situation.

The Hebrews cast lots. We don't know exactly how they did this, but evidently if you wanted an answer from Yahweh to an important question you could take the Urim and Thummim, which were sacred lots or dice, and cast them before a scared ephod (a ceremonial object or garment). Yahweh's "yes" or "no" answer could be read from the way they fell. In rare cases Yahweh would not give any answer at all. This would be like flipping a coin and having the coin stand on edge. If Yahweh would not answer "yes" or "no" it meant that the questioner was cut off from Yahweh because he was displeased for some reason.

We hear a lot about this method of divination in the Books of Samuel, but with the growing sophistication of religion in the prophetic era it seems to disappear. Evidently some method of casting lots hung around though, for when the disciples had to replace the defector Judas they used such a method to decide that God chose Matthias as his replacement.

Most of us are so rational today that we disparage such ancient methods of divination. But the need is still there. There are times in our lives when it is crucial that we make correct choices and have the correct attitude toward a difficult situation. In this respect we are no different than an ancient Hebrew, Roman, or Navajo Indian. The Christian, of course, can

---

1. Frank Johnson Newcomb, *Hosteen Klah: Navajo Medicine Man and Sand Painter*. Oklahoma University Press, 1964, p. 28.

pray and ask for divine guidance, or may even open the Bible at random and with eyes closed place his finger on the page; the verse on which his finger falls is regarded as a divinely inspired answer to his question. Some people today find that the *I Ching* is still a useful means for orienting the ego correctly to life's changing situtations. Though devised many centuries ago this ancient book is wise and profound, and if a person is willing to meditate on its ancient images he is almost certain to receive help. Jungian psychology recommends that we follow our dreams, believing that the Self speaks to us in this way and helps orient consciousness. In spite of our generally rationalistic age, the ancient need for a method of divination lives on— and finds new ways of being met—but not yet enough, and many people flounder because their ego is left stranded in a narrowly rationalistic outlook that keeps them from a vital and meaningful contact with the irrational meaning that is at the heart of life.

So the lot fell to Saul, but no one could find him:

They looked for him but he was not to be found.

Uncertain, they cast the lots again, asking Yahweh:

'Has the man come here?'

In some way we don't understand the lots indicated not only that Saul was there, but where he was:

'There he is . . . hidden among the baggage.'

Sure enough, the people found Saul hiding among the baggage and brought him out, and we are told that as Saul stood among them "he was head and shoulders taller than them all."

Evidently Saul's physical appearance was striking. Even Samuel seems to have been momentarily impressed since he says:

> 'Have you seen the man Yahweh has chosen? Of all the people there is none to equal him.'

And all the people exclaimed:

> 'Long live the king!' (1 Samuel 10:21–24).

It is most remarkable that Saul was concealed in the baggage. Our text says he was hiding—he wasn't simply going about some humble task; he didn't want to be seen. We are forced to infer that Saul didn't want to be chosen king. We can imagine that as Saul watched the sacred lots eliminating other tribes, then other clans, then other families in his clan, he had hid lest the lot by some unfathomable and unwanted act of divine will should fall upon him.

It would be nice to think that Saul hid because of some exemplary modesty in him, but his action went too far for that. The word "modesty" comes from the Latin word "modus" from which our word "mete" is derived. The root meaning of the word is "to take the correct measure." A modest person therefore is a person who takes her correct measure. A modest person doesn't see herself as greater than she is; to do so would clearly be immodest. But neither does she measure herself less than she is—that is equally immodest. If a person has too high a regard for herself we say she is inflated. We react so strongly to the grandiose ideas held by an inflated person that we fail to recognize that a person who thinks too little of herself is also immodest because she also measures herself incorrectly. When a person with inferiority feelings refuses certain tasks that she is called to do because of her supposed inability, this is not modesty but, as we shall see, a form of egocentricity. The truly modest person is centered; she sees herself as she is and measures herself neither too high nor too low. She marks the genuine boundaries of her personality and agrees to those tasks in life to which she is called that fall within those boundaries.

Clearly Saul measures himself too low. His motive for hiding in the baggage is not modesty but an example of his egocentricity. A Nero like Samuel wouldn't be likely to hide as Saul is doing, but a Turtle would. Saul is evidently a Turtle, a man who protects himself from threatening situations by running from them and seeking out some place of refuge where life can't find him. Saul is not willing to meet life head-on and risk himself because he is too concerned with protecting himself from a world that he believes is overwhelming.

The following comment from Fritz Kunkel offers us an interesting contrast between the egocentricity of Samuel and that of Saul:

> The enemy (of God's purposes) is the egocentric form of our own free will which has deteriorated into the will to power or the will to security.[2]

With Samuel it is power; with Saul it is security. This is the difference between the Nero and the Turtle. This is why some of the people refuse to follow him. We are told that after Samuel made his final speech and dismissed the people they all went home except for some "mighty men whose hearts God had touched" who decided to stick around with this strange new king. But others saw Saul as a craven coward. Our text tells us:

---

2. Fritz Kunkel, *Creation Continues*. New York: Charles Scribner's Sons, original edition, 1952, p. 192.

. . . there were some scoundrels who said, 'How can this
fellow save us?' They despised him, and offered him no
present (1 Samuel 10:27).

It's hard to criticize these men who refused to follow Saul.
Who wants to follow a king who hides in the baggage? They
must have wondered why Yahweh chose this man to be king,
and we wonder too. However, as will soon become apparent,
God saw the royal personality in Saul that lay underneath his
egocentric overlay. Kunkel believed that each of us has an egocentric part and a capacity to live from the Real Self. The genuine personality in Saul that came from the Real Self was
kingly, even though it was hard for these men to see it because
it was concealed beneath Saul's Turtle shell. Yahweh made no
mistake when he chose Saul to be the king. While the men who
despised him could only see Saul's craven side, Yahweh saw
through that into the true man. To use words we find later in
the Book of Samuel:

> God does not see as man sees; man looks at appearances
> but Yahweh looks at the heart (1 Samuel 16:7).

In spite of his efforts to avoid it Saul is now officially the
king. Yahweh's will, inscrutable though it was, could not be
changed, and this excessively shy and retiring farmer is now
Israel's first monarch. But Saul hasn't the foggiest idea what to
do. How does one go about being a king? Saul doesn't know,
so he just goes back to his farm in Gibeah and picks up where
he left off. Our text tells us that Samuel dismissed all the people, and "Saul too went home to Gibeah." He acts as though
he hopes the whole business will be forgotten, and the people
act that way too, since to all intents and appearances they just
leave him alone and life in Israel goes on as it did before. But

an event soon takes place that changes all this and reveals the wisdom of God's choice.

The Ammonites, warlike people who lived on the eastern frontier of Israel, laid siege to the city of Jabesh-gilead in the valley on the east side of the Jordan River. The Ammonite king, Nahash, gives an ultimatum to the inhabitants of Jabesh-gilead: Either surrender, in which case everyone will be blinded in the right eye, or they will all be killed. The people tell Nahash that they will make up their minds within seven days, and then in desperation send messengers throughout Israel asking for help. When the Hebrews hear of the plight of their kinsmen they weep—but no one does anything to help. Now this is exactly the kind of emergency that led the people of Israel to ask for a king, but no one thinks to tell Saul what is happening. Or maybe they did think of it but decided that this bumbling fellow wouldn't be of any use even if Yahweh did, in a fit of divine confusion, choose him to be their monarch. As a result Saul is one of the last to find out what is going on, but when he does a surprising thing happens:

> Now Saul was just then coming in from the fields behind his oxen, and he said, 'What is wrong? Why are the people weeping?' They explained to him what the men of Jabesh had said. And the spirit of Yahweh seized on Saul when he heard these words, and his fury was stirred to fierce flame. He took a yoke of oxen and cut them in pieces which he sent by messengers throughout the territory of Israel with these words: 'If anyone will not march with Saul, this shall be done with his oxen!' At this, a dread of Yahweh fell on the people and they marched out as one man. He inspected them at Bezek; there were three hundred thousand Israelites and thirty thousand of Judah. He then said to the messengers who had come, 'This is what you must say to the men of Jabesh-gilead, "Tomor-

row by the time the sun is hot help will reach you." ' The
messengers went and reported this to the men of Jabesh
who were overjoyed; they said to Nahash, 'Tomorrow we
will go over to you and you can do what you like to us.'

The next day, Saul disposed the army in three companies; they burst into the middle of the camp in the last
watch of the night and struck down the Ammonites until
high noon. The survivors were so scattered that not two of
them were left together (1 Samuel 11:5–11).

When Saul hears what the Ammonites plan to do to the
people of Jabesh-gilead he is filled with indignation. He gets so
angry that he forgets all about his own need for security, and
is filled with a tremendous, courageous energy that the Bible
calls "the spirit of Yahweh." In psychological language we
would say that the Real Self came up in Saul and shoved away
his egocentricity. As a result the hero archetype is constellated
in him and Saul's royal personality emerges.

Many people who have been raised in a religious environ-
ment have been taught that anger is bad. After all, St. Paul ad-
monished the Colossians to "give all these things up: getting
angry, being bad-tempered, spitefulness, abusive language
and dirty talk; and never tell each other lies" (Colossians 3:7).
Not only does St. Paul single out anger as something to be
given up, but he places it in bad company, along with lying
and spitefulness. Now depth psychology comes along and tells
us that if we don't express our anger we aren't ourselves. Furthermore, if we repress our anger we split our personality in
two: a conscious side that seems to be good but is actually a
pushover for everyone who wants to take advantage of us, and
a shadow that is dark and angry but has lots of guts.

But Kunkel's psychology helps us by enabling us to distinguish between two kinds of anger: egocentric rage, and anger that comes from the Real Self. Egocentric anger comes
when something threatens our egocentric system of defenses.

Then we may become vindictive, defensive, or fly into a rage. This anger is blind, ignorant, and destructive. But there is also a genuine anger that is the proper response of the human spirit to a situation that has become so outrageous that it offends the deepest part of us. This anger enables us to respond to oppression heroically and creatively, and makes us capable of sacrificial action on behalf of others. This is not blind, stupid anger, but actually heightens our awareness and sharpens our minds. It was this kind of anger that Jesus had when he drove the money changers from the temple, and it is this anger, "the spirit of Yahweh," that now blazes forth from Saul. It is a manifestation of Saul's Royal Self, and when it comes up there is no room for his craven egocentric side.

In the presence of this spiritual anger Saul no longer thinks of himself, but of the people of Jabesh-gilead. His frightened "I" nature, with all its fears for its own safety, is replaced by his "we-Self" that includes his people and himself in a single unitary subject. Now we can see why Yahweh chose this man to be king; it was not a divine mistake, but an example of God's wisdom.

Moreover, Saul's high-spirited and We-centered actions inspire others to a like-minded spirit, and many of the Israelites rally around their inspired leader as he plans the rescue of Jabesh-gilead. Saul's example tells us something important about leadership. The true leader wins the loyalty of others because of who he is. When the Real Self is constellated in someone, others are affected by it. Those still caught in their egocentricity will try to avoid such a man, or even to kill him because his very existence threatens their egocentricity. But there will always be some who are hungry to break free of their egocentric chains and live from their own Centers, and these people willingly follow the inspired leader. There is no need for such a leader to harangue people, to try to be charismatic, or to play a carefully staged role. The genuineness of his personality is enough. By invisible threads it reaches out to others who are like-minded and draws them to him.

Saul's fury is described as a "fierce flame," but as we have said this is not the blind and stupid rage of egocentricity but the inspired spirit that comes from the innermost Center. It fills Saul with cunning and brings out in him his latent ability as a military leader. Saul acts as if he had been leading men to war for years. He assembles his army, organizes it, and appoints his captains. Then he sends word to the people of Jabesh-gilead that help is on the way. They do their part by telling Nahash that on the following day they will surrender. This puts the Ammonite king offguard. Saul then divides his army into three companies and stealthily surrounds the Ammonites. Shortly before dawn the Israelites attack. The surprise is perfect and the rout of the Ammonites so complete that the Israelites

> . . . struck down the Ammonites until high noon. The survivors were so scattered that not two of them were left together (1 Samuel 11:11).

Anyone who understands anything about military tactics will recognize the enormous logistical difficulties involved in mobilizing and organizing an army and then coordinating a surprise attack at night. The story of the battle against the Ammonites is a testimony to Saul's military and organizational abilities.

This victory had an electrifying effect on Israel. As a direct consequence, the kingship of Saul is publicly renewed. The people march to Gilgal for an impressive public ceremony; a sacrifice is made to Yahweh and Saul is proclaimed king all over again as though to banish forever the doubts the people had about him. Saul now demonstrates another quality of his genuine Self: his magnanimity. For the people remember the men who despised Saul and would not follow him, and clamor for their death. But Saul says, "No one is to be put to death today, for today Yahweh has brought victory to Israel" (1 Samuel 11:13).

We can imagine that when Saul forgave his former detractors they became some of his most loyal soldiers, for from this time on the people of Israel exhibit a remarkable loyalty to their king. In Saul's whole long reign not one person ever turned against him no matter how badly things went—except, of course, Samuel. This loyalty was the response of the people to the emergence in Saul of the Real Self, which brought out in him his royal personality, and which the people never forgot even when Saul's egocentricity later returned. They were far more loyal to Saul than they were later to David, whose reign was marked by civil war and inner divisions and whose own son led an insurrection against him. And as we will see, among all the people none were more loyal and grateful than the people of Jabesh-gilead, who at the end of Saul's life find a way to repay him.

At this point Samuel announces his retirement. It's no coincidence that Samuel retired at the moment that Saul truly became the leader of the people: Samuel can't share the stage with his rival. So he retires, in what has to be the most remarkable retirement ceremony the world has ever seen. First Samuel gathers all the people together—he's going to get as much publicity out of this retirement as he can—and then announces to them:

> 'I have faithfully done all you asked of me, and I have appointed a king over you. In the future it is the king who will lead you. As for me, I am old and grey, and my sons are here among you' (1 Samuel 12:1–2).

It's incredible, but evidently Samuel has forgotten that the people don't like his two sons, that their dishonesty is one reason they wanted a king. Samuel acts as though the people should be glad his two sons are going to remain among them. Of course Samuel isn't aware of all this; his image of himself as a righteous man doesn't allow him to acknowledge that he is capable of such a self-serving plot. But plots that are unconscious are more dangerous than plots that are conscious, for as long as they are unconscious they cannot be influenced by our conscious moral values. Moreover, we don't take responsibility for the plots we engage in unconsciously, but do evil with a demonic subjective feeling of innocence and righteousness. Sometimes people excuse the actions of others, saying, "He didn't mean to do it, of course," or "I don't mean to say that he intended it." It's much better to deal with someone who knows and deliberately does something destructive than someone who does something destructive on such an unconscious level that he has no awareness or sense of responsibility for it. In the former case there is at least a psychological self-honesty which makes it possible to deal with that person and hope for change. Small wonder that repentance and confession—which includes making conscious unconcious evil—is the first step on the road to salvation.

By the way, it's interesting to note that we hear nothing more in our story about Samuel's two sons. Evidently once Samuel retired, the people settled things in their own way: by simply ignoring them.

Samuel then proceeds with his speech:

'Here I am. Testify against me before Yahweh and before his anointed. Whose ox have I taken? Whose donkey have I taken? Have I ever wronged or oppressed anyone? Have I ever taken a bribe from anyone? If so I will here and now requite you' (1 Samuel 12:3-4).

When most people retire others praise them. However, Samuel acts as though he might be accused, not praised, so he turns the ceremony into a confrontation between him and the people. This is all very strange since the people have always shown him great respect. The people, who must have been mystified by all of this, hastily reassure him:

> 'You have neither wronged nor oppressed us, nor accepted a bribe from anyone.'

However, Samuel still isn't satisfied. He continues to confront the people like adversaries:

> 'Yahweh is witness against you and his anointed is witness today that you have found nothing in my hands?' (1 Samuel 12:4–5).

Why should Yahweh be a witness *against* the people? There is no need for the existence of this adversary situation because no one has ever attacked Samuel or questioned his integrity. But maybe Samuel has another kind of adversary: within himself. He acts like a man who has a bad conscience about something but has not looked within and taken responsibility for it. Samuel projects his unconscious doubts about himself onto other people. He fantasizes that the people are accusing him because he hasn't faced his own unconscious self-doubts. It's the unresolved problem of his shadow come back again because he hasn't faced it, and this is why he needs an inordinate amount of reassurance. He will also need to find someone to be the shadow for him—and we will see that Saul is elected. The people, who by now are thoroughly confused, are also frightened because this irascible but powerful old man is so displeased with them. They hastily agree:

> 'He is witness' (1 Samuel 12:5).

Now that the people have been coerced into agreeing that Samuel has never wronged them (something they would gladly have told him at the very beginning), Samuel goes on to the next part of his plan: to indict the people once again for wanting to have a king, and, in the process, to make a threat against Saul. First he reviews the unfaithfulness of the people to Yahweh in the past—making it sound as though the sins of their fathers are their sins also—and then he accuses them:

> 'But when you saw Nahash, king of the Ammonites, come to attack you, you said to me, "No, a king must rule over us"—although Yahweh your God himself is your king. Here then is the king you have chosen; Yahweh has set a king over you. If you reverence and serve Yahweh and obey his voice and do not rebel against his order, and if both you and the king who rules over you follow Yahweh your God, all will be well. But if you do not obey the voice of Yahweh, if you rebel against his order, his hand will be against you and against your king' (1 Samuel 12:12–15).

Samuel's ethic is the ethic of obedience. The people are to obey Yahweh, and if they do, all will go well, but if they don't, Yahweh will punish them and King Saul also. Notice that in this short paragraph Saul is referred to four times. Of course he surely was present at the ceremony and heard all of this. It's clear that, according to Samuel, Yahweh is angry that the people wanted a king, and puts up with Saul only as long as Saul and the people obey him. If Saul doesn't obey him, Yahweh's hand will be against him.

There is no love in any of this. The relationship between Yahweh and the people is founded on obedience, not on love, and the relationship between Samuel and the people, which might have been founded on love, likewise rests upon obedience.

The story doesn't tell us how all of this affected Saul, but we can imagine that he took in very carefully everything Samuel said. Later, when Samuel finds a way to accuse him of disobedience, Saul will remember the dreadful punishments in store for those who purportedly disobey Yahweh.

Naturally this is all pretty intimidating to the people. They have no relationship of their own with Yahweh and have to take Samuel's word for it. But just in case they aren't sufficiently impressed, Samuel produces a miracle. He demands that all the people watch carefully. Then he reminds them that this is the dry season of the year. Then he calls upon Yahweh and before the day is out a great thunder and rain storm comes. If anyone among the people wasn't thoroughly cowed before, he certainly is now.

Now that he has reduced the people to Clinging Vines, Samuel can simulate some generosity toward them. So he says in a more kindly vein,

'Do not be afraid . . .'

But lest they begin to take heart too much he quickly adds,

'. . . you have indeed done all this evil, yet do not turn aside from following Yahweh, but serve Yahweh with all your hearts. Do not turn aside after empty idols which, being empty, are useless and cannot save, since for the sake of his great name Yahweh will not desert his people, for it has pleased Yahweh to make you his people. For my part, far be it from me that I should sin against Yahweh by ceasing to plead for you or to instruct you in the good and right way. Only reverence and serve Yahweh faithfully with all your heart, for you see the great wonder he has done among you. But if you persist in wickedness, you and your king will perish' (1 Samuel 12:20–25).

The hapless people can only cry out like guilty little children who are chastised by a frightening "Black Giant" of a parent:

'Plead for your servants with Yahweh your God that we may not die, for we have added to all our sins this evil of asking to have a king' (1 Samuel 12:19).

Notice that the people refer to Yahweh as *your* God. As far as the people are concerned only Samuel has a relationship with Yahweh. This seems to be the way Samuel wants it. He never encouraged anyone else to have a relationship with Yahweh, but kept it all for himself. This way he can be the "Parent" and they are the guilty little children, which guarantees that he will be in the power position. There is nothing of the redeeming feminine qualities of relatedness in Samuel because that would threaten this power position. He is a one-sidedly patriarchal figure who only knows of the severity of Law and can only demand obedience. There is no compassion in him, no spirit of creative compromise, no eros, no nurturing qualities. For him position is all-important and relationship is nothing, and position means power. Any threat to his power and Samuel becomes exceedingly resentful and uneasy, for his Nero egocentricity is based upon it.

But isn't Samuel retiring? Isn't he giving up his power? So we were told, but in fact Samuel doesn't really retire at all. He vanishes from the stage for a while, presumably, as we have mentioned, because he can't stand sharing it with Saul, but he comes back as soon as he sees an opportunity to bring about Saul's downfall. His "retirement" speech in effect sets Saul up perfectly for the destruction that is to come.

3

Ascent and Decline

The defeat of the Ammonites was a great victory for Israel, but the real struggle was to liberate themselves from the domination of the Philistines. Our story now tells us how Saul, with the aid of his courageous son Jonathan, frees his people from the hated enemy. In this struggle with the Philistines Saul's star will shine brightly and his power will be at its height. But even as the sun at midday has already started its subtle descent, so Saul's power begins to decline at the moment of his greatest success. And the one who is instrumental in starting this decline is none other than Samuel.

The Philistines controlled Israel by forbidding them to make weapons:

> There was not a single smith in the whole land of Israel, because the Philistines had reasoned: We must prevent the Hebrews from forging swords or spears. Hence all the Israelites were in the habit of going down to the Philistines to sharpen every ploughshare, axe, mattock, or goad. The price was two-thirds of a shekel for ploughshares and axes, and one-third for sharpening mattocks and straightening goads (1 Samuel 13:19–21).

It was obviously going to be difficult for Saul to build an effective army under these conditions. While he could defeat the Ammonite rabble with skill and enthusiasm, he was going to need more than that to overcome the highly trained army of the Philistines. Saul realizes that he needs a professional army, so he chooses three thousand of the most valorous men from the host he assembled to overwhelm the Ammonites and sends the rest home.

Of course Saul's army is too small to attack the Philistines, so Saul assumes a defensive position and cautiously waits. No doubt he used the time to train, organize, and equip his soldiers as best he could. But war began unexpectedly when his son Jonathan courageously but rashly smashed one of the sacred pillars at Gibeah—symbol of Philistine power in the land of Israel.

Jonathan is the Sir Galahad of our story. In contrast to his father, who had a complicated and tortured personality, Jonathan seems to have been naturally free of egocentricity, one of those rare people who are naturally whole. Unlike David, who could be very egocentric and often had to be reprimanded by God for his actions, Jonathan seems to have been free of selfishness. We can only think of positive things to say about him: he is fearless, self-sacrificing, loving, and generous.

We wonder about Jonathan's mother. In this all-too patriarchal story we hear next to nothing about the wife of Saul, or the wife of Samuel for that matter. It's worth noting that Saul's son, Jonathan, is in marked contrast to Samuel's egocentric and devious sons, and is far more loyal to his father than David's sons ever were to him. If we judge a man by his children, Saul is at the top of the list. Even if much of the credit should go to Saul's wife, at least Saul had the sense to marry a good woman. However, Jonathan's very virtuousness makes him less instructive for us than Saul or David. The truth is that most of us are more like Saul or David than we are like Jonathan. Jonathan we admire. Saul and David teach us.

When Jonathan smashed the sacred pillar the Philistines assumed that the Hebrews were going to revolt. The chances are good that Jonathan did this act deliberately in order to provoke a war. The Philistines responded accordingly and began to assemble an impressive army at Michmash, on the southern border of Israel. From here they could readily invade Israel and subdue these unruly rebels who had violated their sacred symbol of authority. We are told that the Philistines soon had three thousand chariots, six thousand horses, and so many infantry that they were as numerous as the sands on the shore of the sea. This, of course, is an exaggeration, but there can be no doubt that the Philistine army was far more numerous and better equipped than anything Saul could muster.

The Philistines moved quickly. Even before their entire army was assembled three powerful raiding parties set out for nearby Hebrew cities to terrify and subdue the people. The Hebrews were so frightened that many of them hid in caves, holes, crevices, vaults, and wells. The war had hardly begun, but already the situation seemed hopeless, until Jonathan, whose rash bravery had precipitated this crisis, acted again.

Accompanied only by his armor-bearer, Jonathan approached the main Philistine camp at Michmash. Saul, unaware of Jonathan's movements, is encamped nearby at Gilgal. Jonathan meanwhile came up through a pass and close to the Philistine outpost. He then said to his armor-bearer:

'Come on, let us go across to the outpost of these uncircumcised men; perhaps Yahweh will do something for us, for nothing can prevent Yahweh from giving us victory, whether there are many or few of them. . . . Look, we will go across to these people and let ourselves be seen. If

they say to us, "Do not move till we come to you" we shall
stay where we are and not go up to them. But if they say,
"Come to us" we will go up, for that will be the sign for us
that Yahweh has given them into our power' (1 Samuel
14:6–10).

Jonathan wanted a sign from Yahweh before he attacked.
He assumed that Yahweh was listening in on his conversation
with his armor-bearer and that the Philistine response to his
approach would indicate Yahweh's intentions. As Jonathan
and his companion approach, the Philistines say to themselves:

'Look, the Hebrews are coming out of the holes where
they have been hiding.' The men of the post then hailed
Jonathan and his armour-bearer. 'Come up to us,' they
said, 'we have something to tell you' (1 Samuel 14:11–12).

That was the signal for which Jonathan has been waiting.
He and his armor-bearer charge the outpost with swords
drawn and the battle begins. Amazingly, the outpost is defeated, and the Philistine soldiers scatter. Like a wildly spread-
ing infection, the fleeing soldiers spread fear through the rest
of the army. The Bible refers to what happened as "a very
panic of God." When Saul sees that the Philistine army is beginning to disintegrate he quickly attacks with his small but
well-organized army and completes the rout of the enemy.
Our story says, "That day Yahweh gave Israel the victory."
The tale does not end there, however. Saul wants his soldiers to keep pursuing the fleeing enemy, but he is afraid that
when they come upon the Philistine camp they may stop to
loot and feast. So he sends an order through the army that no
one is to eat any food until evening under penalty of death.
However, Jonathan didn't hear about his father's order—perhaps he was too far ahead of the others hotly pursuing the en-

emy—and when he finds a honeycomb that the bees have abandoned he eats some of it. The story tells us that "his eyes brightened," indicating that Jonathan's blood sugar level was low and the honey enlivened him. Refreshed, he pursued the enemy more vigorously than ever. Later one of the soldiers tells Jonathan of Saul's order, but Jonathan boldly defends his action, saying:

> 'My father has done the nation a disservice. See how much brighter my eyes are now that I have eaten this mouthful of honey. By the same token, if the people had eaten their fill of the booty they took from the enemy today, would not the defeat of the Philistines have been all the greater?' (1 Samuel 14:29–30).

Meanwhile Saul is wondering whether to pursue the Philistines through the night or break off the engagement, and he decides to consult Yahweh by casting lots, but when the lots are cast they give no answer. As we have seen, when this happened it meant that Yahweh was displeased about something. So Saul knows that someone must have offended Yahweh in some way and determines to find out who it is by casting the lots again. He says to his soldiers,

> 'Come forward, all you leaders of the people; consider carefully where today's sin may lie; for as Yahweh lives who gives victory to Israel, even if it be in Jonathan my son, he shall be put to death' (1 Samuel 14:38–39).

The lots are cast and it falls on Jonathan. Saul says to his son, "Tell me what you have done." And Jonathan answers, "I only ate a mouthful of honey off the end of the stick I was holding. Here I am. I am ready to die." And Saul replies, "May God do this to me and more if you do not die, Jonathan."

At the time Saul issued his decree he had no idea that the offender would be his son, but now that he knows he does not go back on his word. If it had been any other soldier, that man would have been killed, and Saul does not make an exception because of favoritism to his son. His decree is harsh, but absolutely fair. Unlike Samuel, who played favorites with his sons, Saul is determined to treat everyone in his army equally. But Saul's soldiers will not let Jonathan be killed. They say to the king:

> 'Must Jonathan die after winning this great victory for Israel? Never let it be so! As Yahweh lives, not one hair of his head shall fall to the ground, for his deeds today have been done with the help of God.' And so the people ransomed Jonathan and he was not put to death.

We do not read of any objection raised by Saul to the refusal of the people to carry out his order. He had done the fair thing and all the army saw it, but he was no doubt deeply relieved that his order was not carried out and gladly let the matter drop. As for the Philistines, he decided not to pursue them further, and the remnant of their army returned to their own country.

I have already mentioned that Saul's soldiers were deeply loyal to him. Throughout his long reign, with the exception of a few dissidents who joined David, no one ever rebelled against Saul or was a traitor to him. To a man they followed him through thick and thin. The basis of the soldiers' loyalty to Saul is Saul's loyalty to them. They refused to carry out Saul's order and execute Jonathan, but they saw that Saul was absolutely fair with them. A king who treated everyone in his army exactly alike, not even favoring his own son, was a man to be trusted and followed. Once again Saul's Real Self has come through. The soldiers have seen his royal personality— and they never forgot it.

The story of this victory over the Philistines stretches our credulity. Justifiably we wonder how two lone soldiers could have panicked a whole army. But the Bible gives us the explanation when it says, almost in passing:

> The Hebrews who had earlier taken service with the Philistines and had accompanied them into the camp, themselves defected to the Israelites with Saul and Jonathan (1 Samuel 14:21).

It seems there were Hebrew conscripts with the Philistine soldiers in the outpost that Jonathan attacked, who, inspired by Jonathan's valor, turned upon their Philistine comrades in the heat of the battle. We may surmise that other Hebrews in the ranks of the Philistines did the same thing when they saw the soldiers from the outpost fleeing, with Jonathan and their fellow Hebrews in hot pursuit, and this unexpected defection, plus Saul's timely attack, produced disorder in the Philistines that soon turned into panic.

Saul's victory over the Philistines was followed by victories over Israel's other enemies:

> Saul consolidated his rule over Israel and fought against all his enemies everywhere: against Moab, the Ammonites, Edom, Beth-rehob, the king of Zobah, the Philistines; wherever he turned he was victorious. He did great deeds of valour; he defeated the Amalekites and delivered Israel from the power of their plunderers (1 Samuel 14:47–48).

We are also told:

> Any strong man or man of valour that caught Saul's eyes he recruited into his service (1 Samuel 14:52).

In this way Saul built up a strong military force that successfully protected Israel against its enemies for the next twenty years. But even in the midst of Saul's greatest triumphs an event took place that contained within it the seeds of Saul's destruction. A seed falls silently to the ground. There, unnoticed, it sprouts and sends down the roots that ultimately will produce a plant. So a seed fell into Saul's innermost being and took root, a seed that produced, not a healthy growth, but evil.

To understand what happened we must go back to the situation that existed after Jonathan had smashed the sacred pillar and the Philistines were assembling their powerful army at Michmash. As we have seen, Saul mustered what forces he could and is sitting opposite the Philistines at Gilgal. Both armies are mobilizing rapidly, but while the Philistine buildup continues smoothly the Israelites are frightened; with each passing day more of Saul's soldiers desert and the morale of his troops sinks lower. Good general that he is, Saul realizes that he must attack while he still has an army left, no matter how desperate the odds, but before he can do so a sacrifice must be made to Yahweh, for it would be unthinkable to go into battle without asking for Yahweh's favor. The sacrifice would be a holocaust, a ritual in which the whole sacrificial animal is consumed by fire as an offering to Yahweh, and nothing reserved for the people.

Now Samuel, as we have seen, has supposedly retired, but nevertheless he sent word that he would come and offer the holocaust for Saul and his army. Samuel, who has been living at Ramah, about sixty miles away, told Saul that he would arrive within seven days. Time goes by and Samuel doesn't come. Saul counts the days, but no Samuel. Each day more of his men desert and his army becomes more uneasy. Finally seven full days have come and gone and Samuel has not come. Convinced that Samuel is not going to come Saul makes a fateful decision—he will offer the sacrifice himself:

Saul was still at Gilgal and all the people who followed him were trembling. He waited for seven days, the period Samuel had fixed, but Samuel did not come to Gilgal, and the army, deserting Saul, was dispersed. So Saul said, 'Bring me the holocaust and the communion sacrifices'; and he offered the holocaust. Just as he was completing the offering of the holocaust Samuel came, and Saul went out to meet him and greet him, but Samuel said, 'What have you done?' Saul replied, 'I saw the army deserting me and dispersing, and you had not come at the time fixed, while the Philistines were mustering at Michmash. So I thought: Now the Philistines are going to fall on me at Gilgal and I have not implored the favour of Yahweh. So I felt obliged to act and I offered the holocaust myself.' Samuel answered Saul, 'You have acted like a fool. If you had carried out the order Yahweh your God commanded you, Yahweh would have confirmed your sovereignty over Israel for ever. But now your sovereignty will not last; Yahweh has searched out a man for himself after his own heart and designated him leader of his people, since you have not carried out what Yahweh ordered you.' Samuel then rose and left Gilgal to continue his journey (1 Samuel 13:8–15).[1]

It was not ritually wrong for Saul to offer the sacrifice. While at this point in the history of Israel there may have been hereditary priesthoods, they did not have the exclusive right to perform sacrifices. In fact, priestly offices were often performed by the fathers of a family or the chief of a clan. For instance, we read in 1 Samuel 6:15 that when the Ark of the Lord was brought to Beth-shemesh the men of the city offered

---

1. There is another version of Saul's disobedience, not so favorable to him. See Appendix B for my reasons for favoring the story found in 1 Samuel 13 over the story in 1 Samuel 15.

holocausts to Yahweh.[2] Not even Samuel challenges Saul's right to offer a sacrifice; he only complains because Saul has allegedly disobeyed his order. But Saul *has* obeyed Samuel's order. The biblical text is quite explicit on this point:

> He waited seven days, the period Samuel had fixed, but Samuel did not come. . . .

Only after he had waited the full seven days did Saul act, and his intention was not to usurp Samuel's place as priest but to save his army from disintegration.

All the time that Saul was anxiously waiting, Samuel was dawdling along for some unexplained reason, even though he must have known that each day he delayed things got worse for Saul and his soldiers. When he does arrive he offers neither an explanation nor an apology for his tardiness, nor does he display the slightest interest in Saul's problem. Instead he uses the situation he himself had created as a pretext for accusing Saul of disobeying Yahweh and concludes by putting what amounted to a curse on him.

Samuel's behavior is extraordinary, but there is an explanation: it is all a setup motivated by Samuel's smoldering resentment, and fueled by his unwillingness to turn over his power and influence to another man. Saul was the victim of a plot—whether it was entirely conscious to Samuel or partly an unconscious plot doesn't matter, for the results are the same.

Saul was "mouse-trapped." In football the offensive guard sometimes pulls out of position when the ball is snapped. The defensive lineman opposite him is drawn through the hole in the line his opponent has left, and then zap! an offensive back hits him from the side, clearing the way

---

2. A later editor has inserted verse 15a that refers to Levites attending the service, but this is a much later extrapolation.

for the ball-carrier to charge through the gaping hole. This play is called a "mouse-trap" and this is what happened to Saul. He was meant to perform the holocaust and then, just when he did, Samuel could come in and accuse him of disobedience.

Saul is shocked when Samuel pronounces judgment on him; evidently he expected Samuel to be reasonable and understanding. It seems clear enough to Saul why he had to act as he did; why isn't it that clear to Samuel? Or why, at least, isn't Samuel willing to hear him out? It won't be the last time that Saul comes to Samuel asking for understanding and receives rejection and judgment instead.

Saul knows why he performed the sacrifice when he did, and he understands all too well the consequences of Samuel's judgment. But he doesn't understand the psychological significance of the action he undertook when he performed the holocaust on his own: at that moment Saul became his own person and reached for his own relationship with Yahweh. We have already noted that the people referred to Yahweh as Samuel's God, and that no one had any relationship with Yahweh except Samuel, but when Saul acted on his own he took a step out of the collective psychology of his people and toward his own individuation. Without intending it, Saul had made an individual decision and reached out for individual consciousness. It was a fateful step, a move forward from which he cannot retreat except at grave peril to his soul.

Jesus once said, "Once the hand is laid on the plough, no one who looks back is fit for the kingdom of God" (Luke 9:62). Once a person achieves a modicum of psychological growth and awareness he is severly punished by the unconscious if he reneges on it and sinks back to his previous level. It is better never to see anything than to have our eyes opened and then decide to be blind again. When we turn our back on a step we have taken toward individuation, the inner forces that were ready to be helpful and creative turn dark and destructive. But, as we will see, Saul does just that. He has no choice now but to finish what he has started and be his own person—Samuel and the Philistines and the general level of unconsciousness of his people notwithstanding. But the effect of Samuel's pronouncement is to paralyze Saul, and turn him away from his own development and back to a regressive attempt to protect his ego.

As long as Saul was faced with outer crises he continued to act heroically from the Real Self, risking himself on behalf of his people. But once the outer situation was taken care of, and the enemies of Israel defeated, Saul lapsed back into his latent egocentricity. Samuel has told him God is going to replace him, and Saul is consumed with anxiety over his fate and the desire to save himself at all costs. The result is that he loses his royal personality, and his old egocentric personality takes over again. Only now his egocentric form is that of the Nero—he has touched too much power to remain a Turtle. Saul wants the security that comes from dominating others rather than the security that comes from hiding, but the bottom line is the same: he is just as egocentric as he was before; he has gone back on the personal development he had acquired.

As long as we are egocentric we live with a sense of threat. Samuel has constellated that sense of threat in Saul, and as a consequence Saul becomes consumed with anxiety. He can dominate everyone about him but he is himself dominated by the frightening fantasies of personal destruction that invade his consciousness. Samuel's seed grows into a dangerous paranoid complex that repeatedly engulfs Saul in dark depression and stark fear.

4

The Evil Spirit from Yahweh

Saul has been successful in everything he has undertaken. The Philistines have been sent scurrying back to their own land, the other enemies of Israel have been laid low, and the people are delighted with their king. Now that there are no more battles to be fought Saul is surely entitled to rest, relish his well-deserved victories, and enjoy himself. But this is not to be the case, for now that the outer battles are over the inner battle begins, and this is a battle that Saul doesn't know how to fight.

It sometimes happens that when we are involved in outer crises the inner crises seem to disappear, but when the outer life is in order the unconscious stirs up the latent difficulties and forces upon us our unresolved psychological problems. In our culture, for instance, we have the idea that if we can only resolve our outer problems everything will be all right. Usually this means acquiring enough success and wealth. However, rich people are as likely to develop psychological difficulties as anyone else. No amount of outer success can shield us from the necessity of individuation.

51

This is particuarly true of men who have achieved worldly success at the expense of their inner development. Just when such a man has accomplished his long cherished (but egocentric) goal a dark spirit may be constellated within him that fills him with bad moods, anxious forebodings, and obsessive ideas. Behind all this darkness is the anima, the name we give to a man's feminine side (as we noted toward the end of Chapter One) and who personifies his unconscious personality.

Of course a man in this situation seldom realizes that his unhappy state of mind is thrust upon him because his unconscious personality is rebelling against his ego-centered life and goals. He only knows that he feels bad, and just as he once thought he would be happy if he only achieved his outer goals, so now he supposes that his unhappiness is due to outer problems. Consequently he blames his depression on other people, the unfortunate state of the world, the fact that the wrong political party is in power, etc. But behind his depression, boredom, psychosomatic symptoms, or increasing reliance on alcohol or drugs is something like an inner woman who is angry because he has ignored his soul and forsaken the feminine values of life, and who will torture him vengefully until he does an about-face.

Kunkel sees this inner woman at the heart of the parable Jesus tells in Matthew 13:33: "The Kingdom of heaven is like the yeast a woman took and mixed in with three measures of flour till it was leavened all through." Kunkel says of this parable:

> How many of us have felt her (the woman in the parable) hands kneading the dough, penetrating the very core and substance of our life? Whenever we suffer and ache from outer or inner pain, whenever nightmares from within or evil actions from without disturb our peace, we can be

sure that these are the hands of the woman who prepares us for the leaven of the Kingdom.[1]

There is a point to this torture. Robert Johnson, in his book *HE!*, a psychological study of the legend of the Holy Grail, gives us a good example of it. Parsifal, hero of the legend, has an opportunity to find the Holy Grail which alone can heal the land of its ills, but he has forgotten his quest while achieving knightly successes. He is now at the apex of his career and a great feast is given in his honor in Arthur's court. At the height of the celebration and congratulations in walks "the hideous damsel." This is a woman who is so ugly and repulsive that at the mere sight of her the celebrating knights are stopped cold, their revelry replaced by sudden gloom. The hideous damsel walks up to Parsifal and recites a list of his sins. In detail she tells him of all the acts he might have done but failed to do, and of all the people who have been made to suffer by him as he made his way to personal power and success. Pointing her finger at him she says, "It is all your fault." By the time the hideous damsel is through with the knights they all slink away back to their knightly tasks, and Parsifal is sent off to resume his quest for the Grail Castle, which is symbolic of his individuation.

Johnson writes of the appearance of the hideous damsel in the court:

> This is the hideous damsel. This usually happens at the very apex of a man's career, at the time of his greatest success. He has just been named president of the corporation, has just been elected to the academy, has just made his first million, or whatever the apex of life is for him, and within three days the hideous damsel will walk in on him.

---

1. Kunkel, *Creation Continues*, original edition, 1952, pp. 192–93.

> This is the *anima* gone absolutely sour and dark.
> There is some correlation between the amount of fame and
> adulation one gets in the outer world and the condition of
> the *anima*. They often have an inverse relationship to one
> another. When a man really makes it, then he is often in
> for one hell of a time with his *anima*.[2]

Johnson points out the inverse relationship between the
amount of fame and adulation a man gets in the outer world
and the condition of the anima. Jung had the same thing in
mind when he said that a man's anima compensates his persona. That is: if a man's outer face in the world (the persona) is
powerful and successful, the face the unconscious turns toward him (the anima) overpowers him from within with dark
moods and forebodings.

It would be more accurate to say, however, that the anima
compensates a man's egocentricity. There is nothing wrong
with the persona until our egocentricity distorts it. We all need
to turn a certain face to the world (the persona) in order to project and make effective our personality in interactions with
other people and outer reality. But if our egocentric goal is to
have worldly power or glory, this proper role of the persona is
distorted to egocentric posturing. If we are successful in this
egocentric striving we will achieve the desired power over others, but the anima compensates our outer power by dominating us from within. We may indeed rule corporations, or be at
the pinnacle of professional success, but we are helpless to do
anything about the moods, fears, and somatic complaints that
rule us from within. No matter how much adulation or power
we succeed in getting for ourselves we will not be able to rid
ourselves of "the hideous maiden," that is, a nagging sense of

---

2. Robert Johnson, *HE!*. King of Prussia, Pa.: Religious Publishing
Company, 1974, p. 75.

threat, and disturbing, guilty feelings that somehow something is wrong.

This is the way psychology looks at the experience of Saul. He is a man who has won his outer battle, but now must face his inner battle. If he turns his back on the demands of his soul she will turn against him and possess him with fearful moods. However, the Bible states the problem in surprising language:

> Now the spirit of Yahweh had left Saul and an evil spirit
> from Yahweh filled him with terror (1 Samuel 16:14).

Are we to understand from this biblical quotation that God is the source of evil? Anyone from a Christian tradition will be shocked at such a thought.

In the Old Testament the answer is "yes." The Old Testament has an unflinching monotheism. There is only one God and everything that happens comes from him, whether it is good or evil. Later Jewish popular thought, which we find reflected in the New Testament and early Christianity, relieves God of the burdensome responsibility for evil by invoking a devil who opposes God's will and is the cause of illness, sin, and death, but in the Old Testament there is no Satan to relieve God of blame.[3] So the prophet Amos says,

> Shall there be evil in a city, and the Lord hath not done it?
> (Amos 3:6 KJV).

And in Isaiah we read:

> I am the Lord, and there is none else. . . . I form the light,
> and create darkness: I make peace and create evil: I the
> Lord do all these things (Isaiah 45:5 and 7 KJV).

---

3. There are only four references to Satan in the Old Testament. None are important and all are late in origin.

Depth psychology says Saul's problem is due to anima possession; the Bible says it comes from God. Chrisitianity says evil comes from Satan, but the Old Testament says this evil spirit comes from Yahweh. How are we to resolve the difficulties?

In war there is a general who gives orders to his soldiers who carry them out. If we are attacked by our enemy's forces we experience his soldiers, but we know that somewhere behind the movements of the soldiers is the opposing general. In a game of football, the coach sends players into the game, and may even call the plays himself. If we are the opposing team we experience the players opposite us, but at the end of the game the newspapers will refer to the "winning" or "losing" coach.

These images give us a rough picture of the structure of the psyche. Beyond the ego is the world of the collective unconscious, which consists of all the archetypes, those basic building blocks of the psyche that are like patterns of energy that shape our life and profoundly influence consciousness. The archetypes are inner images charged with power and purpose. The shadow and the anima or animus are examples of the multitude of inner images that make up the powers of our inner world. But beyond all the archetypes is the Self, the image of God in the soul. It is as though each of the inner powers is connected to the Self, and the energy that they possess comes from the Self. The images of the unconscious are thus powers through which the energy of the Self moves and flows. Trace any archetypal power back far enough and you get to the Center. In religious language we would say that God uses the archetypal energies of the unconscious for a divine purpose.

This is why, in our present state of knowledge, the proper model of the psyche is both "polytheistic" and "monotheistic." On the one hand, the psyche is a multitude, a polytheism, as it were, of seemingly independent archetypes each with its own personality and function. They correspond to the gods and goddesses of polytheistic mythology such as, for instance, that of ancient Greece. On the other hand, the psyche has an inner core, a point of unity. We call this the Self or the Center, and it seems to be the ultimate source of psychic energy and purpose. Because of this inner unity we need a monotheistic model—the many is reduced to its source in the One.

In Jungian psychology at the present time there are those who emphasize the unity of the psyche and those who emphasize its diversity. Jung himself, while recognizing the seemingly autonomous nature of the archetypes, never doubted the fundamental unity of the psyche in the Self. There are those, however, who stress the multiplicity of the psyche to the point where the reality of the Self appears to be greatly diminished or even denied, and who refer to their psychology as "archetypal psychology" in order to distinguish it from Jung's original "analytical psychology."

The followers of archetypal psychology point to Greek mythology as the best paradigm of the psyche, and with good reason, for Greek mythology offers a rich portrayal of the multitude of archetypes that influence our consciousness and shape our lives. But even the ancient Greek sometimes spoke of "God," signifying his belief that all of the deities of the Greek pantheon were part of one vast divine being. As Greek scholar Walter F. Otto put it,

> Despite very great diversity in character and temperament, these gods all possess the same nature. Hence they are regularly contrasted to the human race as a unity; it is 'the gods' who determine the human lot, and frequently enough the poet (Homer) says simply 'god' or 'the diety,' as if, in the final analysis, it were only a single power that affected earthly existence from above. . . . The gods

whose spirit is perceptible in every happening operate
partly individually and independently of one another and
partly in combination as a unity.[4]

Those who emphasize the unity of the psyche point to the
biblical image of the deity, and stress the Bible's insistence that
there is only one God. But even the New Testament described
a multitude of quasi-autonomous spiritual agencies, which St.
Paul called "principalities and powers," and told stories of an-
gels who often carried out God's will for him. So while Greek
mythology stresses multiplicity, and the Bible unity, both
point to the paradox that the psyche is many and one at the
same time.

In Saul's case we can say that an autonomous archetypal
power—the anima—has him in her grip, but behind the anima
is the Self. In religious language we would say that the ultimate source of Saul's problem is his lack of relationship with
God. This is why the biblical story can say that the "evil
spirit" comes from Yahweh. But our inquiry cannot stop here,
for how can it be that God is the source of an *evil* spirit?

Both Jung and Kunkel pointed out that the Self has a dark
side. In the Bible, this dark side is contained in the image of
the wrath of God, and the idea that the fear of God is the beginning of wisdom.

The Bible has many stories of the dark side of God. One
excellent example is the story of Balaam the prophet, found in
Numbers 22, which Rivkah Sharf Kluger discusses so well in
her book *Satan in the Old Testament.* The Hebrews are coming
through the desert from Egypt to Canaan. They have defeated
the border kingdoms and are approaching Moab. Balak, the
Moabite king, is afraid, and sends for the prophet Balaam to

---

4. Walter F. Otto, *The Homeric Gods*. Thames and Hudson, 1954, pp.
127 and 170.

come and prophesy against the Hebrews, which would amount to putting a curse on them. Balaam rides his donkey toward Moab but three times the donkey inexplicably turns off suddenly from the path. Enraged, Balaam beats his donkey and starts out again until finally:

Then Yahweh opened the eyes of Balaam. He saw the angel of Yahweh standing on the road, a drawn sword in his hand. . . . And the angel of Yahweh said to him, 'Why did you beat your donkey three times like that? I myself had come to bar your way; while I am here your road is blocked. The donkey saw me and turned aside from me three times. You are lucky she did turn aside, or I should have killed you by now, though I would have spared her' (Numbers 22:32–34).

Balaam, properly impressed, then enters into a discussion with the dark angel of God. He learns from the angel that he can go to Moab, but can only prophesy what God tells him to prophesy. Now that his ego is in accordance with the will of God, Balaam is allowed to proceed on his way.

It is this dark side of the Self that Kunkel says is responsible for the sense of threat or feeling of pressure that bedevils so many of us. The threat may be projected onto the outer situation—inordinate fear of financial collapse, the loss of a relationship, some illness, or communism—or it may be a vaguely defined but overwhelming sense of inner anxiety. When we look at the sense of threat from our egocentric point of view it looks like a devil to us. We think *we* are all right, and the pressure is the dark reality that must be eliminated. If we look at the situation from the point of view of the Self, however, *we* are the problem, and the threat is the only way to teach us what is wrong and must be corrected. This is why "the dark side of God" must be faced.

Kunkel points out that when we pursue false (egocentric) goals we are bound to feel the pressure. It is "life exacting the penalty for the violation of its laws."[5] The Self turns against us because we are blocking life and its creativity; it seeks to destroy our egocentricity so creative energy can flow again, and will destroy us in the process if we resist. As long as we don't understand this we react incorrectly by trying to shore up our defenses and find a way to avoid the pressure. Inevitably we will then think the enemy is outside of us, as Saul did, when the real enemy is within. As we noted earlier, Kunkel said of this enemy that it is the egocentric form of our free will that has become the will to power or the will to security.

In Saul's case, the threat was that he would lose his throne, someone else would have the power, and he would be destroyed. He saw the reason for this anxiety entirely outside of himself: Yahweh had chosen someone who, even now, might be plotting against him. As long as he looked only outside of himself he failed to see his inner enemy: his egocentricity. The only way out for Saul is to turn and face the threat, but this is what he cannot yet bring himself to do. As long as he can't, he must necessarily experience the dark side of God, "the evil spirit from Yahweh."

Like Balaam, Saul's way through life is blocked by the dark side of God. The anima, who conjures up Saul's dreadful fantasies, can be thought of as God's agent, a "dark angel" sent to turn Saul aside from his egocentric way and onto the path of his individuation. The "spirit from Yahweh" is evil in the sense that it will destroy him unless he changes. It is an expression of the ruthlessness of the Self that destroys everything that isn't fit to exist. It is not, however, absolute evil. Absolute

_____

5. *Fritz Kunkel: Selected Writings.* New York: Paulist Press, 1984, p. 187.

evil would be a purposeless destructiveness, a power that would destroy the good without meaning or purpose.

When Saul faced his outer enemies he needed courage, the capacity for decisive action, firm resolve, and extraverted energy. If he is to face his inner world he will still need courage; he will also need an introverted focus, psychological insight, and the capacity to accept the irrational side of life with its paradoxes and subtleties. In the inner realm he will discover that he cannot overcome his difficulties by imposing his will upon the unconscious, but can achieve his purpose only through understanding, negotiation, and relationship with his feminine side and the other point of view that she embodies.

However, Saul remains extraverted. When a person can only function in an extraverted way it is a symptom of egocentricity. As Kunkel put it:

> . . . the egocentric consciousness is necessarily extravert. The Ego is interested first of all in its own defense. Therefore it watches the outer world to anticipate dangers, and to find weapons. And it cannot allow itself to turn inwards. It would discover that it has no independent reality and that it is only part of a larger unity. But the belief in its independence and self-sufficiency is the basic factor of its existence.[6]

Our story continues:

> Saul's servants said to him, 'Look, an evil spirit of God is the cause of your terror. Let our lord give the order, and

---

6. Fritz Kunkel, *In Search of Maturity*. New York: Charles Scribner's Sons, 1946, p. 95.

your servants who wait on you will look for a skilled harpist; when the evil spirit of God troubles you, the harpist
will play and you will recover' (1 Samuel 16:15–16).

Saul's courtiers realize that the king is ill and hope that if
a skilled harpist plays beautiful music Saul's depression will
lift and he will be well again.

Contemporary mental health practitioners would surely
agree with the conclusion of Saul's servants. Today Saul's condition might be diagnosed as a depressive state with marked
paranoid tendencies. The aim of the treatment would be to
eliminate the depression, elevate the mood, and ease the paranoid fears. The standard psychiatric book *Diagnostic and Statistical Manual of Disorders* would probably assign Saul's case the
diagnosis "Major Depressive Disorder no. 296.3." "Common
associated features include depressed appearance, tearfulness,
feelings of anxiety, irritability, fear, brooding, excessive con-
cern with physical health, panic attacks, and phobias."[7] Mood-
elevating, antidepressant drugs would be the treatment of
choice, possibly with ego-oriented therapy as an adjunct. If
the treatment succeeded in relieving the patient of his symptoms it would be regarded as a cure.

However, we are now in a position to see that in Saul's
case the depression and fears are not the illness but the symptoms of the illness, and that the real illness is Saul's egocentric
state which has deviated so far from his Real Self that symptoms have been produced in an attempt to cure him. The cure
for Saul would be the dissolution of his egocentricity and the
reorganization of his personality around his inner Center; then

---

7. *Diagnostic and Statistical Manual of Mental Disorders* (DSM III). American Psychiatric Association, 1981, p. 211.

the symptoms, no longer necessary, would disappear of their own accord. Saul's former sterile life could be replaced by a creative life, and his morbid concerns over his fate would be replaced by a feeling for his common humanity with others.

This is the way a religious psychology looks at such an illness. The symptoms are not the illness, but the signal that something is fundamentally wrong, and the stimulus to seek a cure. The Self produces the symptoms in rebellion against the egocentricity of the ego. While various palliatives might temporarily relieve the symptoms the underlying problem remains, and the symptoms tend to reappear until a fundamental change in personality takes place. This is why Jung once said that we never cure a neurosis, but maybe it eventually cures us. If this statement is contrasted with a conventional attitude toward illness we can see that it amounts to a kind of Copernican revolution when it comes to our ideas of what constitutes illness and health.

This is also why we tend to resist being healed. Even when we go to doctors or other healing practitioners for help there is a secret and deep resistance toward being truly healed because such a healing requires us to give up our egocentric attitudes. This seems to us like death. At the same time that we complain of our suffering we hang on like grim death to the cause of it—our precious ego. For the problem is that if we get well we have to act well, and acting well means giving up our egocentric ways.

Of course Samuel played a role in all this because he was the one who planted the seed in Saul that has developed into his depression. But Samuel, while contaminating Saul with his unconscious plots and resentments, could not have affected Saul if he had been healthy to begin with. Only because Saul had not worked through his egocentricity was he vulnerable to Samuel's pronouncement of doom. Suppose for a moment that

Samuel had said what he did to Jonathan instead of to Saul. Jonathan had a naturally healthy ego. Samuel's attack on him might have troubled him but it wouldn't have made him sick. If he had been in Saul's place he might have said to himself, "That old man is going too far this time. He should have stayed retired where he belonged. Where the hell was he anyway all this time while my army was disintegrating in front of my eyes? If he had cared about us he'd have shown up on time. Now when it's too late he arrives and tries to blame me. Well, I'll have none of that!"

To continue with our story:

> Saul said to his servants, 'Find me a man who plays well and bring him to me.' One of the soldiers then spoke up. 'I have seen one of the sons of Jesse the Bethlehemite' he said; 'he is a skilled player, a brave man and a fighter, prudent in speech, a man of presence, and Yahweh is with him.' At this, Saul sent messengers to Jesse, saying, 'Send me David your son who is with the sheep.' Jesse took five loaves, a skin of wine and a kid, and sent them to Saul by David his son. And so David came to Saul and entered his service; Saul loved him greatly and David became his armour-bearer. Then Saul sent to Jesse saying, 'Let David enter my service; he has won my favour.' And whenever the spirit from God troubled Saul, David took the harp and played; then Saul grew calm, and recovered, and the evil spirit left him (1 Samuel 16:17–23).

When the king's courtiers suggest a harpist be called Saul agrees. This indicates that Saul knows something is wrong with him, but accepts a method of treatment that won't require him to change. Like many people today who go to healers we want to find someone who will "do something" for us— pray for us, give us a psychological program to follow, perform surgery or prescribe medication. We want to be cured of our pain but not healed.

So it's decided to find a musician and someone knows just the man: David, one of the sons of Jesse. David comes, and when he plays his harp, sure enough, Saul becomes calm and the bad mood leaves him for the time being. David, moreover, is a gifted, graceful, handsome youth and Saul loves him greatly.

Our storyteller tells us his story with such brevity that we may miss the profound irony of this event: It is David whom Saul invites to the court, who temporarily cures the king, and whom Saul loves more, perhaps, than anyone else in the world. But this very David is the man Saul dreads, the feared one chosen by Yahweh to take his place, the terrifying enemy in Saul's dark imagination.

We are likely to be so entranced with the picture of the beautiful youth David playing his harp and curing the king that we may fail to notice the fact that the courtiers don't call a doctor but a musician. Ordinarily when someone is ill a doctor of some kind is summoned. Ancient people had many doctors, healers, and specialists in various kinds of cures just as we do today, and there has never been an ancient people without their healers—except the Hebrews. That's the reason the courtiers don't call a doctor: there isn't a physician worth calling. In the whole of the Old Testament there is only one reference to a doctor attending a patient and that is a disparaging one. We find that in 2 Chronicles 16:12: faithless King Asa had sore feet, and "he turned in his sickness, not to Yahweh, but to doctors." Where are the wise women who are experts at finding healing herbs? the shaman or shamaness who at great risk goes into a trance in search of her patient's lost soul? the man who knows how to put broken bones back together or bind up a bleeding wound? or the scientifically trained physician such as could be found in ancient Greece? They are all missing in the Old Testament.

One explanation is that in most cultures the gods selected certain people who had a special relationship with the spiritual world and commissioned them to be healers, but in the Old Testament when Yahweh chose a particular individual and made a unique relationship with him it was to be a prophet. A prophet speaks to the moral and theological issues of his day and tries to lead the people as a whole spiritually, but he is not a healer for the individual. The divine energy that made many people healers in other cultures made them prophets in the culture of ancient Israel.

A second explanation, offered by Paul W. Walaskay of the Presbyterian School of Christian Education,[8] has to do with the Hebrew conception of illness. For most ancient people illness had a natural physical or spiritual cause; therefore there were doctors who looked to nature for the cause of the problem in the hope of finding the cure. The word *physic*, which means "nature" and from which the word physician is derived, is prominent in Greek literature but does not occur in the Old Testament. In the Old Testament illness doesn't come from natural causes, but from God himself. If you are afflicted it is God who caused it. Therefore if you wish to be healed your only recourse is to turn to God. That is why the Chronicler said disparagingly of King Asa that when he turned to physicians he "turned not to Yahweh." Unfortunately, God didn't seem to be very interested in healing people, and the

---

8. See the article, "Biblical and Classical Foundations of the Healing Ministries," by Paul W. Walaskay, Ph.D., Dean of the Faculty, Presbyterian School of Christian Education, Richmond, Virginia, found in the September 1983 edition of *the Journal of Pastoral Care.*

stories of healings in the Old Testament are extremely rare, mostly limited to extraordinary miracles performed by Elijah and Elisha.

I would like to add a third explanation: that the lack of a feminine element in the Old Testament generally, and in Yahweh's character particularly, precluded an interest in healing. Yahweh is a patriarchial deity par excellence. Even when we take into account the Old Testament passages concerned with Sophia, such as we find in Proverbs 22, we are still left with the overall impression that Yahweh is one-sidedly masculine. But healing requires an admixture of the feminine element, if by the feminine element we understand the principle of relatedness. For instance, the health of the body calls for the proper relatedness of all of its various components, and also for a healthy relatedness of body and soul. In the healing arts the effective therapist, physician, or spiritual healer needs to have a certain positive relatedness to the patient and vice versa. Where such a relatedness is present a certain kind of healing energy flows between them; without it spiritual and psychological healing work cannot progress. It is also the feminine element that endows individual life with meaning. In the Old Testament the main emphasis is upon corporate life, and the life of any given individual is insignificant. In the New Testament the feminine element is reintroduced with Mary, Jesus, and the many women who accompanied Jesus, and there we find healing stories abound.

We are left then with a desperate situation: a king who is sick, but has no physician, who welcomes a passive form of treatment via the music but does not know how, or is unwilling, to commit himself to an active effort to get well. Even in ancient Israel, however, there was, as we have seen, a way to be healed: a person could seek out God, and if he found him, then God, the author of all illness, just might heal him. We must remember that when Saul offered the sacrifice at Gilgal he took an important step toward his own individual relationship with God. Now if he is to recover his health he must continue the journey that he began at that time. Even though Samuel has declared that Yahweh has rejected him, Saul must try to seek out Yahweh and make his own relationship with him. In psychological language, there is no way for Saul to go but to individuate. It makes no difference that individual development away from the collective was almost unknown among his people at this time. There had been spiritual pioneers—Jacob, Rebekah, Joseph, Moses—who individuated. Saul must be one too.[9]

So it was David who came to heal the king and not a physician. David plays his harp and sings his songs so beautifully that the king recovers from his dark moods, for music, since it proceeds from the creative Center, has a certain healing power. But Saul's illness goes too deep to be cured by music. He suffers from a complex that must be pulled up by the roots like a weed, and from a disorientation of the ego that must be fundamentally changed. David's music is to Saul like fresh paint to a crumbling building: for a time things appear to be better, but the rotten structure lies within and the reconstruction must be from the inside out. In fact, as we will see, Saul's demonic complex will soon begin to destroy the relationship with his healer, David, whom Saul, initially, loved so much.

Meanwhile David, who is quite a Star it would seem, becomes a favorite with the people. It becomes apparent that he has many abilities besides his ability as a musician, and he is soon appointed to be an officer in Saul's army, for Saul was, as we will remember, always looking for capable people for his

---

9. See my book, *The Man Who Wrestled with God*. Ramsey: Paulist Press, 1983.

armed forces. David demonstrates the military abilities for which he was later famous and quickly becomes one of Saul's most prominent captains. His very success, however, ultimately doomed his relationship with the king, as is clear from the next part of our story.

5

Saul's Plots

Our story continues:

On their way back, as David was returning after killing the Philistine, the women came out to meet King Saul from all the towns of Israel, singing and dancing to the sound of tambourine and lyre and cries of joy; and as they danced the women sang:

> 'Saul has killed his thousands,
> and David his tens of thousands.'

Saul was very angry; the incident was not to his liking. 'They have given David the tens of thousands,' he said 'but me only the thousands; he has all but the kingship now.' And Saul turned a jealous eye on David from that day forward.

On the following day an evil spirit from God seized on Saul and he fell into a fit of frenzy while he was in his house. David was playing the harp as on other days and Saul had his spear in his hand. Saul brandished the spear; 'I am going to pin David to the wall' he said. But David twice evaded him.

Saul feared David, for Yahweh was with him but had turned away from Saul. So Saul dismissed him from his presence, making him commander of a thousand; he marched at the head of the people. In all his enterprises David was successful, and Yahweh was with him. And seeing how well he succeeded, Saul was frightened of him. But all Israel and Judah loved David, because he was their leader in all their exploits (1 Samuel 18:6–16).

Saul is jealous. Jealousy is one of the egocentric emotions; it occurs when someone else has what *we* want. Jealousy can destroy friendships, undermine marriages, corrupt families, and even incite people to crime and murder. When jealousy goes this far the egocentricity of the ego is involved—we want what we want and will go to any lengths to get our own way. Then the egocentric emotion of jealousy becomes the door through which evil enters the soul.

As with all egocentric emotions it's not so easy to overcome jealousy once we are in its grip. For instance, suppose that we say to ourselves, "Jealousy is bad. It means I'm egocentric. So I won't be jealous. I'll put it away from myself and refuse to stoop so low." Our jealousy then promptly goes underground (not very far underground) while we pretend to ourselves that we are above such things. The jealousy-free pose we strike is as egocentric as the jealousy because it isn't genuine, but a pretense we have adopted. When we are "bad" we can't solve the problem by banishing the badness and pretending we are "good" because a feigned goodness is as egocentric as the badness.

Fortunately there are several positive steps we can take when we are jealous. We can learn from it what it is that we really want. Let's say we hear that an acquaintance has just published her first novel. Maybe we even congratulate our acquaintance, but are aware that our words of congratulation sound hollow because the fact is that we are jealous. At such a moment we are likely to feel bad about ourselves. Why can't we be big enough to rejoice with this person who has won a well-deserved reward for her strenuous efforts? But we are all too aware of our low, mean thoughts—"It was just luck; she didn't deserve it" . . . "It isn't a good novel, just trash, and was only published because people read trash." Perhaps we need to know we are jealous because *we* want to write and publish a novel. Remember that we are only jealous when someone else has what we want. For the most part, when we want something badly there is in our wanting an admixture of egocentric desire and the genuine longing of the Self for expression. When we are jealous of our writer friend the chances are it's because we have a writer in ourselves who isn't getting expressed. To be sure, our ego is in there too wanting the praise and glory and maybe money, but the urge to write is from the Self and is genuine. It's not only the ego that's ambitious. The Self also is "ambitious" because it wants expression. When understood, our jealousy can lead us to a deeper awareness of the Self and its creativity.

We can also talk with our jealousy. The technique of dialoguing with parts of our personality is called "active imagination" by C.G. Jung and is a way to come to terms with the unconscious. The technique comes from the premise that our personalities are not unities, but consist of many relatively autonomous parts. However, with most of us, there is a definite ego that can act as a center of consciousness and a kind of psychological clearinghouse. By personifying the different parts of ourselves the ego can "talk" with various parts of the psyche.

A convenient place to begin active imagination is by talking consciously with a part of ourself that is already talking with us. Take jealousy, for instance. We are already hearing from our jealous personality—all those mean, churlish thoughts that enter our screen of awareness spontaneously and uninvited are from "the jealous one" within us. To do active imagination we need to listen to these thoughts, then reply to them, just as if we were talking with an actual person; then listen to what the jealous part of us answers, and in this way continue a dialogue for as long as we wish or as long as the dialogue remains alive. It usually helps to write down the dialogue while it is in progress or after it is over; this gives it reality and enables us to refer back to it later if we wish to do so.

In active imagination both the ego and the part of ourselves with which we are dialoguing have equal status. We are not out to suppress this part of ourselves, even though it might be unpleasant to us; we want to be fully awake, alert, and hold to our own position.

It's impossible to predict how any dialogue will turn out, just as it is impossible to predict how a dialogue with another human being will turn out. The hope is, however, that by dialoguing we can work something out within ourselves. It often does happen that after doing active imagination we somehow feel more unified than we did before.[1]

We can also pray about jealousy. The proper kind of prayer might be a kind of confession, in which we frankly share our jealous thoughts with God. However it's important not to indulge in self-condemnation, for self-condemnation only keeps our egocentricity alive. In our prayer we are not asking God to banish these jealous thoughts outright, but to help us understand them and find a creative solution to them.

We can also confess our jealous thoughts to the other person. This is not always an appropriate step to take, of course, but often it works surprisingly well, especially when we are jealous of a friend. Jealousy is never more regrettable than

---

1. The last chapter of my book *Healing and Wholeness* includes a more complete description of active imagination.

when it occurs between friends. When we are jealous of a friend something has intruded into our relationship that is petty and potentially destructive to the friendship. Sometimes it is possible to admit to our friend our jealous feelings: "You know, when I heard you were going to have your novel published I have to admit that while I was happy for you I was also jealous." Such an honest confession of our feeling may eliminate the jealousy. It's as though the bigness of our sharing with our friend eliminates the littleness of our jealousy and our friendship is, accordingly, intact once more. To put it in more psychological language: the action of sharing, which comes from the Real Self, transforms the jealousy that comes from the egocentric ego. Notice, however, that the jealousy is never transformed by trying to deny or repress it. It can only be transformed when it is openly acknowledged in some way—to ourselves, to others, or to God.

Saul might have resolved his jealousy if he had gone to David and shared it with him in this way. He could have said, "You know, I was happy that you were so successful, but when I heard the women praising you more than they praised me I must confess that I was jealous."

As I have already mentioned, David is a bit of a Star. If Saul was also a Star, we would have the dangerous situation of two Star egos occupying the same stage. Jealousy is the almost certain result of such a situation, and confession of the jealousy is a possible cure. However, Saul is not so much a Star as a Nero and there is a deeper egocentric emotion in him than jealousy: fear. True, Saul no doubt would like the praise that David is receiving, but his biggest need is for power, and his great fear is that someone else will take his power away from him and he will be destroyed. This is why, when Saul hears the women praise David, he says darkly, "He has all but the kingship now."

Saul's paranoid complex creates the brooding fear that he

will be rejected by Yahweh, replaced on the throne and destroyed, and David's success puts David squarely in the path of Saul's complex. Saul has been profoundly disturbed by dark fantasies of his destruction, and David is now in the center of them. Of course this changes and disturbs Saul's relationship with David.

Until now Saul loved David. Love lives between people when the relationship is an expression of the Self; where the Self is, there love is. But as soon as a person relates to another person egocentrically, love vanishes. As long as we are egocentric we only see others in terms of our egocentricity. A Clinging Vine, for instance, will see others as his supporters or as the hateful people who refuse to prop him up. If other people allow Clinging Vine to cling to them he seems to love them—but it is only egocentric satisfaction, not genuine love. Star will evaluate other people in terms of whether or not they admire her. Admirers will be rewarded with smiles and approval, and this may seem like love, but it is only an egocentric reward given to people who do what we want them to do. Detractors will be cordially hated. Turtles will tolerate those who allow them to remain hidden from life's demands, and look with fear on those who insist on pulling them out of their shells. Neros will tolerate those who submit to their power, but hate and fear those who refuse to be dominated. Sometimes, to be sure, like-minded egocentric people join together in a group based (secretly of course) upon the mutual support of their egocentricity, and such a group displays what looks like love and loyalty. But it too is dedicated to the ego, and is what Kunkel called "the Associated Egos." Genuine love, which the New Testament called agape, only exists when it is the Self, not the ego, that determines the relationship.

The situation is made worse by David's continued success. According to the theological notions of the day, success was a sign of divine favor. If someone was loyal to Yahweh and obeyed him, Yahweh would reward him with success. If a person was disloyal, Yahweh would punish him. Turn this around and it follows that if someone is successful it means he is a favorite of Yahweh. David was successful, so Saul was bound to conclude that Yahweh was favoring him. When Saul looked at this through his egocentric concerns for himself he had to conclude, "Is it not clear that Yahweh is with David? David is successful as no one before him. The women sing his praises and give him more glory than they give to me. He is only a step away from becoming the king in my place. I hate him. He must be destroyed." Once again we see how evil enters through the door that our egocentricity leaves open.

Indeed, from this time on Saul seeks David's death. The Bible first tells us the story of how Saul tried to murder David:

> An evil spirit from Yahweh came on Saul while he was sitting in his house with his spear in his hand; David was playing the harp. Saul tried to pin David to the wall with his spear, but he avoided Saul's thrust and the spear stuck in the wall. David fled and made good his escape (1 Samuel 19:8–10).

When Saul hurled his spear at David it wasn't a premeditated act, but a "crime of passion." However, he missed, and that is an important part of the story. An experienced soldier like Saul was surely an expert spearsman, and David couldn't have been sitting far away from him, but Saul missed because his murderous intention was betrayed from within. When we are contradicted from within, our conscious actions do not succeed. If we consciously intend to do good, for instance, but have not dealt with our inner evil, our good intentions will not succeed. But the opposite is also true: if we decide to do something bad, but have a genuinely good nature within us, the genuine part of us will keep us from being a successful bad man. So Saul's better side keeps his worst side from succeeding. Even apparently hardened criminals may be tripped up by their unconscious decency which sees to it that sooner or later they fail and get caught. This is why Kunkel once said with his typical wry humor:

> To be a good burglar, one must be a bad man. There are very few good burglars, and none of them are perfect. There may be a very few bad men, and possibly not one of them is entirely bad. Thus—sooner or later—every burglar will make a mistake; his unconscious longing for goodness will frustrate the most ingenious crimes.[2]

Such things happen all the time. A teenager gets involved with drugs, but manages to leave the evidence around for his parents to find, or even gets caught by the police . . . A man goes out secretly on his wife, or a wife on her husband, but somehow manages to leave a revealing note in a coat pocket or on the top of the bureau . . . A dictator orders the secret execution of opponents, but somehow word leaks out, or later the graves are discovered.

Saul's rage at David displays all the qualities of an egocentric emotion. First, it is excessive. David has done nothing to justify Saul's anger; the excessive quality of the emotion indicates that it has an egocentric basis. Second, Saul's rage possesses him. A genuine anger that comes from the Real Self motivates us but doesn't possess us. When Saul was angry at the Ammonites who were besieging the people of Jabesh-gilead he was filled with great energy but he wasn't possessed; hence he was free to act with a cool head and a clear mind. Egocentric emotions, on the other hand, leave us more or less

---

2. Kunkel, *In Search of Maturity*. New York: Charles Scribner's Sons, 1946, p. 7.

stupid. Finally, Saul's underlying motivation is to protect his ego, and any emotion that has that as its basis is bound to be egocentric.

Our story tells us that after Saul threw his spear and missed he tried a more subtle way to dispose of his enemy. Quite likely we are dealing with two different versions of how Saul tried to kill David. Each one is instructive.

When Saul threw his spear at David in an act of hot passion it was terrible but at least it was understandable and human. In the story we now hear, Saul acts coldly, and his coldness is more brutal and repelling than his passion. All ordinary human decency seems to have vanished as Saul devises a plan that not only will lead to David's death but will use his own daughters as the instrument of his purpose.

Saul has become an instrument of evil. The question asked of both psychology and religion is: Whence comes evil? A little while ago, when we discussed Saul's jealousy, I mentioned in passing that our egocentric emotions and attitudes are like a door through which evil enters the soul. Now we need to examine more carefully what this means.

Jung never made his position with regard to evil very clear, but sometimes he seemed to suggest that the Self was as much evil as it was good. If this is the case then the urge to do evil comes from the Self and is an ineradicable part of human nature. We can then only hope that the ego is decent enough and conscious enough to hold off the evil urges and choose the good.

Kunkel, however, had a different view. He always described the Self as a positive force. He never called it "good," for that is usually a human judgment (do we always know what *is* the good?). However, he called the Self creative, which means it can't be evil because, as we saw earlier, absolute evil is by definition a purely destructive force. Evil doesn't come from the Self but from the egocentricity of the ego. It's the ego that is "condensed darkness," and the secret is that the ego is the devil. Of course he means the egocentric ego, not the ego itself. When purged of its egocentricity, the ego properly serves the Self. In religious language the ego then fulfills God's will, but as long as it is egocentric it deviates from God's will.

Kunkel's idea is biblical. God is good and has created a good world, but humankind sins. The psychological understanding of sin is egocentricity. When the ego is egocentric it necessarily sins because it will always "miss the mark," to use the New Testament image for sin. Presumably, God allows this egocentricity to develop because God values free will so highly. He could create perfect, sinless people, but they would not be free. Redemption is a higher state than blamelessness.

However, the New Testament also seems to refer to an evil power that operates independently of the individual human consciousness. In psychological language we would say that there appears to be an archetype of evil apart from the ego. This power for evil, however, does not result in moral or psychological evil unless the ego allows it in. That is why I made the statement that evil enters through a door into the soul that our egocentricity leaves open. To quote Jesus' words:

> Obstacles are sure to come, but alas for the one who provides for them (Luke 17:1).

Nevertheless, if Kunkel is right, this is not a force of absolute evil, nor does this force for evil exist apart from God's purposes. In some way that we do not understand God uses evil for his purposes too. Kunkel writes:

> But if we accept, tentatively, the hypothesis that God's will is fulfilled even while the evildoer moves to destroy

creation, we reach for a moment the 'third point' looking at the murderer and his victim from a higher plane. We see vaguely, as in a fog, how God achieves His ends through His enemies too.[3]

and

If we could decipher the hieroglyphs of history, we should read His name everywhere, in victory and defeat, in war and peace, in suffering and joy. But we cannot see the whole; therefore we misinterpret the parts.[4]

Somehow, then, according to this view, God allows evil to exist because it too is part of a plan which we can only glimpse from our limited human perspective. When we do sometimes see the evil in our life from a larger perspective it is quite a revelation. This is what Joseph told his brothers in the famous story in the Book of Genesis. Joseph is now the prime minister of Egypt, and his brothers, who sold him as a slave years before, are afraid because they are now completely in his power. But Joseph reassures them. Referring to what they did to him, Joseph makes this profound statement about the paradoxical relationship of evil to God's purposes:

Ye thought evil against me; but God meant it unto good (Genesis 50:20 KJV).

Or, in the Jerusalem Bible:

───────

3. Fritz Kunkel, *Creation Continues*, original version, 1952, p. 95.
4. *Ibid.*, p. 117.

The evil you planned to do me has by God's design been
turned to good.

What is not part of the divine plan is that we remain egocentric. According to this point of view, the possibility of our
becoming egocentric must be allowed, or else free will, that is,
individuation, would be impossible. But it is not allowed that
we remain this way. To the contrary all the vital forces of creation—expressed through the reality we awkwardly call the
Self and the images of the unconscious through which the energy of the Self is expressed—are arrayed against it. When we
persist in our egocentricity, evil enters, a genuine evil that is
truly destructive and can never create, an evil capable of the
phenomena of Dachau and racial genocide. For egocentricity
is no small matter. It is not a minor defect of character, but a
fundamental destructive phychological twist that causes our
nature to deviate from its true purpose and fall prey to possession by evil.

So it is with Saul. Whatever now possesses him it is his
egocentricity that has allowed it in, and motivated by his egocentric purposes Saul now plots murder, plans to use his own
family as tools for his evil plans, lies and betrayals. He doesn't
care that he is planning to destroy a man who is innocent, a
previous benefactor, one who is loved and needed by his people. Saul is only concerned with the security of his ego and the
furtherance of his dark ambitions.

Saul's oldest daughter is Merab and his youngest is
Michal. Saul will now use them against David. He feigns affection again for David, and to demonstrate it promises to give
Merab to David in marriage. Of course, to marry the king's
daughter was a marvelous thing for a young man like David, a
guarantee of a position of favor and prominence in the kingdom. But Saul adds one proviso: David must prove himself

worthy by going to battle once more against the Philistines. Saul muses:

> Let it be not my hand that strikes him down, but the hand of the Philistines (1 Samuel 18:18).

David is deeply moved that Saul would offer him his daughter in marriage. Trustingly he goes to war, but contrary to Saul's expectations he returns unscathed and victorious. Saul is shaken, but reneges on his promise. We read:

> . . . when the time came for Merab the daughter of Saul to be given to David, she was given in marriage to Adriel of Meholah.

Saul's first plot fails, but he tries again. This time he will use his daughter Michal for his purposes, for Saul is told that Michal has fallen in love with David:

> Now Michal the daughter of Saul fell in love with David. When Saul heard this he was pleased. He thought, 'Yes, I will give her to him, but she will prove a snare for him and the hand of the Philistines will strike him' (1 Samuel 18:19–21).

Saul secretly instructs his servants to tell David that finally the time has come when he should become the king's son-in-law. David is again overcome that a man from a humble position in life such as his should be given the king's second daughter in marriage. Saul then instructs his servants:

> 'Tell David this, "The king desires no settlement except a hundred foreskins of the Philistines, for vengeance on the king's enemies" ' (1 Samuel 18:25).

Of course Saul anticipates that David will be killed in such a hazardous undertaking, but David, delighted and undaunted, promptly goes out, performs the feat, and again returns unscathed. In fact, the situation is made worse for Saul, for we read:

> The leaders of the Philistines went out to battle, but every time they went out to battle David was more successful than all Saul's officers, and his name was held in great honour (1 Samuel 18:30).

Saul's second plot fails. This time Saul cannot renege on his promise and David is married to Michal, but Saul is still driven to kill David. Subtle means having failed he now sends assassins to watch the house where David and Michal are living and to kill him in the morning. David appears to be unaware of his danger, but, our story tells us, Michal is alert:

> That same night Saul sent agents to watch David's house, intending to kill him in the morning. But Michal, David's wife, warned him, 'If you do not escape tonight, you will be a dead man tomorrow.' Then Michal let David down through the window, and he made off and took to flight and so escaped.
>
> Michal then took the teraphim, laid it on the bed, put a tress of goats' hair on its head and covered it with a garment. When Saul sent the agents to arrest David, she said, 'He is ill.' Saul, however, sent the agents back to see David, saying, 'Bring him to me on his bed for me to kill him.' So they went in, and there on the bed was the teraphim with the tress of goats' hair on its head! Then Saul said to Michal, 'Why have you deceived me like this and let my enemy go, and so make his escape?' Michal an-

swered Saul, 'He said to me, "Let me go or I will kill you" ' (1 Samuel 19:11–17).

It must have been hard for Michal to decide between her father and her husband, but she loves David so much that she doesn't hesitate to make her choice even though she knows that her father may kill her when he finds out that she helped David escape. We can't help but admire her; she's clearly the heroine of this part of our story. On the other hand, David is shown in a negative light. He seems only to be thinking about saving his own skin and shows no indication that he cares about Michal's safety or is grateful to her for risking her life to save him.

We have already suspected that David's egocentricity is that of the Star. It's a typical failing of such people to assume that other people exist for their benefit. The story of David and Michal illustrates the differences we pointed out earlier between genuine love and egocentric pseudo love. Michal acts out of genuine love, from what Kunkel called "We-feeling," and so she is able to act sacrificially. David has egocentric emotions toward Michal, and consequently perceives her in terms of his own need.

We don't hear much more about Michal until the sixth chapter of the Second Book of Samuel. The story we find here is extraneous to the story of Saul, but worth commenting on. David now is the king. The Ark of the Lord is being brought back to Jerusalem and David leads the procession. He dances in front of the Ark and gets so carried away that he winds up dancing virtually naked in public. All present applaud the king, and if they have any misgivings over his dancing naked through Jerusalem they keep it to themselves. Michal, however, lets David have it when he returns to the palace. She says to him,

What a fine reputation the king of Israel has won himself today, displaying himself under the eyes of his servants' maids, as any buffoon might display himself (2 Samuel 6:20–21).

A pretty tactless statement, but no doubt there's some truth to it. David, however, takes offense and becomes so defensive and angry that he apparently rejected Michal from that time on, for the Bible tells us that to the day of her death Michal had no children. This is how Stars can act when people refuse to be their admirers but tell them the truth as they see it.

6

David

The focus of our story now shifts to David. The similarities and the contrasts between Saul and David are instructive. History likes to remember only the good things about David, but the fact is that David could do as much evil as Saul. We have already seen that David's treatment of Michal is highly questionable, but his treatment of the priest Ahimelech leaves us in no doubt about David's capacity for self-serving actions; his darkest side emerges in the story of the use he made of the generous but unfortunate priest.

David fled from Saul so suddenly that he had no provisions and no weapons with him, so he went to Nob, where he was known to the priest Ahimelech. David arrives alone, and under such strange circumstances that Ahimelech can't help but be suspicious. So David reassures the old man with a lie:

> 'The king has given me an order and said to me, "Let no one know anything of the mission I am sending you on, nor of the order I am giving you." As regards my soldiers, I have arranged to meet them at such and such a place. Meanwhile, if you have five loaves of bread to hand, give them to me, or whatever there is' (1 Samuel 21:2–4).

David is something of a con man. A con man takes you in by making his first statement something you believe. Once you believe the first statement you are likely to believe the second, and if you believe the second, you are well on the way to swallowing the whole story. When David tells Ahimelech that Saul has sent him on a secret mission he has said something believable, for everyone knows that David is Saul's right-hand man. The fact that David arrived with no provisions whatsoever and no weapon either must surely have aroused Ahimelech's suspicions, and David's cursory explanation that he is going to meet his soldiers later on doesn't help very much. But since Ahimelech believed the first thing David said he pushed his doubts aside. Besides, the kindly Ahimelech wants to believe David. He's like a loving parent whose son gets into mischief and gives the parent devious explanations for his behavior. The parent wants so badly to believe that his son hasn't done something really bad that he accepts the explanations without question.

David must have had his doubts too—doubts about what he was doing to Ahimelech. But he pushed these into the unconscious in order to maintain his image of himself as a glorious person. Successful Stars are so used to having people admire them that they make the mistake of thinking they actually are admirable people, and overlook their own darkness, but, as we will see, when David was through with Ahimelech the priest was not applauding any longer.

Taken in by David's opening statements Ahimelech explains to him that the only food available is the consecrated bread that is set aside for ceremonial purposes. To take this would be roughly analogous to a good Roman Catholic's taking the consecrated host from the tabernacle, but David doesn't hesitate to accept it even though Ahimelech reminds him that his soldiers shouldn't eat it unless they have kept themselves from women. To overcome this objection David has to tell another lie, which isn't surprising, for once we tell one lie it usually takes a second lie—or a whole series of them—to back up the first. He says,

> 'Certainly, women are forbidden us, as always when I set off on a campaign. The soldiers' things are pure. Though this is a profane journey, they are certainly pure today as far as their things are concerned' (1 Samuel 21:5–7).

So David receives the consecrated bread. But he also needs a sword. Ahimelech tells him that the only weapon available is the sword of the slain Philistine giant Goliath that has been kept at the sanctuary at Nob. So David takes Goliath's sword too and continues his flight. However, he has been seen. Doeg the Edomite, a servant of Saul, overheard the conversation between David and Ahimelech. David saw Doeg out of the corner of his eye but didn't do anything about it, presumably because he was so anxious to be on his way.

I once read a sermon—who preached it I can't recall—in which the minister pointed out that when David took the sword of Goliath he took up evil, for Goliath was an evil man. We can't do something evil without becoming evil. Some people suppose they can get into evil and not become contaminated, but that isn't possible. In fact, as the British writer Laurens van der Post once pointed out, we tend to become like the evil that we oppose. This is what makes war so psychologically dangerous; even when we go to war to oppose what we believe to be evil, we can't help but become partly evil ourselves. When David takes Goliath's sword it means that he intends to oppose Saul's evil with evil of his own. An old saying goes, "He who lies down with dogs gets up with fleas." Evil has this kind of contaminating effect and David gets a bad case of it. David has saved his body, but now he is in danger of losing his soul. Why he didn't lose his soul we will see later in our story.

David leaves Nob and continues his flight to the Cave of Adullam. When word gets out that David is an exile he is joined by many of the discontented people of the country:

> All the oppressed, those in distress, all those in debt, any-
> one who had a grievance, gathered round him and he be-
> came their leader. There were about four hundred men
> with him (1 Samuel 22:2).

It would be nice to think of David as a kind of Old Testament Robin Hood, but the truth is that the Cave of Adullam was a well-known stronghold for robbers, and David's retinue is a motley crew of social misfits that must have contained many unsavory elements.

Later in our narrative we learn that David and his men live by extortion. Chapter 25 of 1 Samuel tells the story of David and Nabal. Nabal is a wealthy man with a beautiful wife named Abigail. When David and his men come upon him they offer to "protect" his flock in return for a handsome reward. The crotchety Nabal refuses, and David decides to kill him. When Abigail sees David coming she goes to meet him and with presents and abject flattery persuades David not to kill her husband. Nabal's life is spared, but when Nabal realizes how close he came to being murdered he is so shocked that he dies anyway, presumably from a heart attack. David doesn't waste any time grieving; he promptly takes Nabal's wealth and his wife Abigail as well.

All of this puts David in a dark light, but the worst is still to be told. After David left Nob, Doeg went to Saul and told him everything. Saul sent for Ahimelech and accused the honest old man of treachery. Ahimelech pleads his innocence: he didn't know that David was running away from the king, and believed that David was on a secret mission for him. Anyone in his right mind would have known that a man like Ahimelech was telling the truth, but Saul isn't in his right mind. Angrily he gives the order that not only Ahimelech, but every living creature in Nob is to be destroyed: men, women, children, cattle, donkeys, sheep—all are to be killed. The order is so heinous that Saul's officers refuse to carry it out. Doeg then steps forward and offers to be the executioner:

> The king said to the guardsmen who were standing beside him, 'Step forward and put the priests of Yahweh to death, for they too have supported David; they knew he was making his escape yet did not tell me.' But the king's servants would not lift a hand to strike the priests of Yahweh. The king then said to Doeg, 'You step forward and strike the priests.' Doeg the Edomite stepped forward and struck the priests himself, that day killing eighty-five men who wore the linen ephod. As for Nob, the town of the priests, Saul put it to the sword, men and women, children and infants, cattle and donkeys and sheep (1 Samuel 22:17–19).

Only one of the priests was not killed: Abiathar, a son of Ahimelech, who managed to escape and find his way to David.

The whole story is sordid. Saul became so mired in his egocentric fears that he plotted murder, used his own daughters, and executed a whole town of innocent people. But David isn't that much better; because he was only trying to save his own skin he brought death to many others. Yet later in Israel's history David was a great hero, and to this day is remembered as the forefather of the Messiah. Why should God favor such a man? A clue is given us in the story of David's reaction when Abiathar told him that Doeg had executed Ahimelech and the other innocent priests. After listening to Abiathar's story David says to him:

> 'I knew that day, when Doeg the Edomite was there, he would be sure to inform Saul. I am responsible for the death of all your kinsmen. Stay with me, have no fear, for he who seeks your life seeks mine too; you will be safe with me' (1 Samuel 22:22–23).

"I am responsible," says David. Only a person who is psychologically honest can make such a statement. Psychological honesty is the ability to be honest with ourselves about ourselves. Psychological honesty doesn't mean that we are "good," but it does mean that we have the courage to confront and acknowledge our reality. Kunkel says that such honesty "is the basis of all the other virtues."[1] Without psychological honesty we will never outgrow our egocentric attitudes; it is the *sine qua non* for individuation. Egocentricity is always a kind of lie, and psychological honesty is the painful antidote. David was not a great person because he was good, but because he was honest.

It is essential that we see our darkness in concrete instances, not just in a general way. We may make a "general confession" in church, or even to our analyst when we say something like, "Of course I know I'm not perfect, but . . ." This isn't enough. Our darkness must be seen and acknowledged in particular acts, in actual relationships, in specific failures. Only then does it become real to us, and only then is our acknowledgment of our darkness sufficiently painful that some of our egocentricity dies.

---

1. Fritz Kunkel, *In Search of Maturity*. New York: Charles Scribner's Sons, 1946, p. 8.

When David acknowledged his fault he did what neither Saul nor Samuel did, and this is why he grew as a person and they remained locked into their rigid attitudes. David also did what Jonathan didn't do. Jonathan was so pure that he seemed to lack a dark side. People like Jonathan are beautiful spirits, but they don't reach the depth of personality development that the Davids of this world reach precisely because they don't have to go through the inner moral struggle and turmoil.

When David was at Nob he was in a very unconscious state of mind, and in this state of unconsciousness his "good" side and his "bad" side were all mixed up. David was bad enough to start the trouble, but too good to do a good job of it. As we have noted, basically good people bungle it when they do something wrong because their good side trips them up. David was too good a person to relish the task of running his sword through the eavesdropping Doeg, but paradoxically, under these circumstances, this "goodness" was a weakness. If David had been more conscious he would have said to himself, "What I'm going to do is a terrible thing; I could get Ahimelech into a lot of trouble." Then when Doeg showed up he would have been ready to see his deviltry through to the end and destroy the potentially treacherous enemy.

As for Saul, he appears to have sunk into utter moral depravity. As we have seen, his order to execute Ahimelech and the others is so evil that his own men won't carry it out. Still, they don't desert him, or betray him by defecting to David's side. They remember the Royal Self in Saul, even though it is now obscured by his demonic egocentricity, and for this reason they remain steadfastly loyal to their soul-sick king.

Saul now hunts for David in his wilderness stronghold. Round and round they go, but though Saul pursues David relentlessly he can't quite catch him. While Saul is on one side of the mountain, David manages to be on the other side.

The pace is exhausting, and Saul and his men, commanded by his general, Abner, make a bivouac. David observes them from a distance and when night comes he and his companion Abishai slip down to the camp and make their way through the dozing sentries to Saul who is asleep on the ground. Beside Saul's head is his spear and a pitcher of water; David and Abishai take them and slip away from the camp. When dawn comes David holds up the spear and pitcher and calls out to Abner:

'Abner, will you not answer?'

Abner replies,

'Who is that calling?'

David answers him,

'Are you not a man? Who is your like in Israel? Why did you not guard your lord the king then? Some man of the people came to kill the king your lord. What you did was not well done. As Yahweh lives, you all deserve to die since you did not guard your lord, Yahweh's anointed. Look where the king's spear is now, and the pitcher of water that was beside his head' (1 Samuel 26:14–16).

Then Saul recognizes David's voice and says,

'Is that your voice, my son David?'

David answers,

'It is my voice, my lord king. Why does my lord pursue his servant? What have I done? What evil am I guilty of?

May my lord king now listen to the words of his servant:
if Yahweh himself has incited you against me, let him accept an offering; but if men have done it, may they be ac-
cursed before Yahweh, for now they have driven me out
so that I have no share in the heritage of Yahweh. They
have said, "Go and serve other gods." So now, do not let
my blood fall to the ground out of the presence of Yahweh; for the king of Israel has gone out in quest of my life
as a man hunts a partridge on the mountains' (1 Samuel
26:17–20).

David is alarmed because Saul's pursuit is forcing him to
leave Israel, and, according to the beliefs of the day, Yahweh
was so closely connected to the land of Israel that if a person
left the land he would no longer be in Yahweh's presence. Saul
is profoundly moved when he realizes that David could have
killed him but spared his life. He replies sincerely:

'I have sinned. Come back, my son David; I will never
harm you again since you have shown such respect for my
life today. Yes, my course has been folly and my error
grave.' David answered, 'Here is the king's spear. Let one
of the soldiers come across and take it. Yahweh repays
everyone for his uprightness and loyalty. Today Yahweh
put you in my power, but I would not raise my hand
against Yahweh's anointed. Just as today your life counted
for much in my sight, so shall my life count for much in
the sight of Yahweh and he will deliver me from all dis-
tress.'

Then Saul said to David,

'May you be blessed, my son David! You will do great
things and will succeed.' Then David went on his way and
Saul returned home (1 Samuel 26:21–25).

This powerful story shows both David and Saul at their best. David is magnanimous. Lesser people would have seized the chance to avenge themselves by killing the sleeping Saul. David could then probably have also seized the throne for himself. But his loyalty and love for Saul are too great, and David does not yield to these ambitions.

Saul is moved by the love, loyalty, and forgiveness that emanate from David's rich and genuine personality. When one person acts from the Center others are also affected. It is not what we *do* that affects others; it is what we *are*. A person who lives from the Center will either make enemies of others, or affect them deeply and positively. Some will be too threatened. They will know in their hearts that this person will compel them to change, just as in chemistry one element is necessarily changed when another element comes into contact with it. Resistance is created because it is in the nature of egocentricity to be rigid, and from this rigidity comes enmity.

But Saul is affected positively by David's love and generosity. This not only shows the greatness of David's true personality, but also the greatness of Saul's. Saul, as we have seen, has sunk into evil, but underneath is his big personality. David's greatness brings out Saul's greatness. When Saul says he has sinned and asks for David's forgiveness he means it; it is Saul's psychological honesty coming through. And when he reassures David of his love for him and promises never again to try and hurt him he is sincere.

Nevertheless David doesn't return with Saul. We are not told why, but we may surmise that David had too much psychological understanding to do so. He knew that Saul was sincere, but he also knew that Saul could not be trusted to stick to his purpose because he was not a whole enough person. It takes more than a temporary conversion or renewal of good intentions to root out evil. David sensed this, and realized that

Saul's need to kill him will return. Wisely David goes his own way.

Of course it is wild fancy, but it is interesting to speculate how a contemporary analyst or spiritual director might have helped if Saul had come to him. Saul would first have told the therapist about his symptoms. There would have been a catharsis as Saul shared his dark and dreadful moods and the awful fears that possessed him. Such a cleansing of the soul through an outpouring of suffering would have helped Saul; at least for the moment he would have felt better now that another human being knew about his burden. Such sharing would also have clarified in Saul's mind that this was a condition that he wanted to get over, and this would have strengthened his faith and resolve. If he felt a good connection with the therapist he would also have felt stronger because he now had an ally—an ally, by the way, whose supposedly more whole and integrated personality would positively affect the tortured patient.

But such a confession alone would not be enough. The sickness in Saul went too deep and a wise therapist would have recognized that they must get to the bottom of the matter if there was to be a cure. So the therapist might ask for a history of Saul's condition. Saul would go back through his life recounting events that led up to his present painful state of mind, and sooner or later the story about Samuel and his prophecy of doom would have come up. This would have been the first time that Saul had told anyone of this frightening event. To take another human being into his confidence would have strengthened Saul and he would no longer have been alone with his awful memories. He might now be able to consider what Samuel had said more objectively, and face more consciously what it meant to him. This might have helped Saul feel so much better that the therapy might have ended right there. Sometimes there is only room for one person in our fearful fantasies, and when a second person is included the nightmarish fears come to an end.

When a process of psychotherapy seems to be going well, with a good flow of energy and good trust between therapist and client, but the presenting symptoms do not recede, it is usually an indication that the unconscious of the client is calling for him to "go the whole way," that is, that complete consciousness and development is called for. In Saul's case, this might now have required him to go back in memory to his childhood. His childhood situation would then be recalled and analyzed. His relationships with his mother and father would be particularly important. An attempt would be made to see how the egocentric qualities of his parents and other significant adults affected the child Saul and forced him into his own egocentric patterns in order that his injured ego might defend itself.

Such an exploration of his childhood would not by itself dispel the egocentricity of the adult Saul, nor would it banish his egocentric fears, but it would add another dimension to his awareness and help him understand more completely his reactions to present life situations. All of this would strengthen his ego in a constructive way and offer the possibility of an expanded range of options when faced by difficult problems.

I mentioned strengthening the ego, and this is as good a place as any to point out that the opposite of egocentricity is not a weak ego. To the contrary, individuation requires a strong ego. Only a strong ego can face its darkness and carry the burden of individual growth. In contrast, a weak ego becomes egocentric in order to protect itself.

Helpful though it is, a reductionist approach by itself does not suffice to bring about a healing. Even though the origin of our difficulties may be traced back to the past, their resolution must take place in the present. The healing comes from a surrender of our egocentricity and a contact with the inner world and its abiding archetypal images that can connect us to the Self. At this point dreams help, because they emanate from the Self and contain healing images. In his hypothetical therapy, Saul could now begin to remember his dreams, record them, and share them with the therapist in an effort to relate to them and understand them.

If Saul ventured into the world of his dreams it would be evidence of a certain amount of courage and faith, for there is never any predicting what our dreams will be like, and no certainty that they will not make us extremely uncomfortable. Sometimes our dreams are frightening; often they are puzzling and leave us perplexed. Since dreams tend to illuminate the dark corners of our souls and fill in the gaps in our understanding of ourselves, we can expect that Saul would encounter in his dreams aspects of himself he might prefer to ignore. But dreams also reveal and relate us to the helpful forces, the inner guiding figures that know the way. Saul certainly would find these helpful forces also, for he is unaware, not only of his own darkness, but also of his true Self.

At first Saul might complain because he has to pay attention to such things as dreams, for their helpfulness is not always immediately apparent to an ego that is looking for quick relief from painful self-imposed symptoms. The dreams will not cure us until we are ready to be cured, but they do have a cumulative effect that gradually alters the contents and quality of consciousness. As Cathy said to Nellie Dean in *Wuthering Heights:* "I've dreamt in my life dreams that have stayed with me ever after, and changed my ideas; they've gone through and through me, like wine through water, and altered the colour of my mind."[2]

Dreams work on us the way dripping water works on stone. One drop may not seem like much, but many drops over a long period of time eventually make a deep impression. Under the influence of dreams the ego slowly comes to realize that it is not the master of the house, that there is a greater power within who speaks through the dreams and must be acknowledged and respected. In this way our egocentric attitudes can slowly be worn away by paying attention to our dreams. To be sure, we find ourselves compelled to pay attention to our dreams and the inner processes they portray. But in this servitude to the Self there is, paradoxically, freedom for the ego, while the supposed freedom of the egocentric ego that goes its own way paying heed to no power other than its own demands is in fact slavery.

Of course this is all fancy. Saul had no therapist to whom he could turn, and there was no such thing in his day as depth psychology. Healing, however, is always a possibility. The therapist herself, for instance, knows that she does not heal, that the healing lies within the client. Even though Saul had no healer to whom he could turn, the power of healing was there within him, for life itself is always the great healer, the divine power works through everything that crosses our path, and the power of the Self is always within us seeking to make us whole.

When David spared Saul's life, and their two souls met and loved each other again however briefly, Saul had a chance once more to be healed. The Self is perhaps never evidenced more strongly than when it is manifested between two people in the form of a love that is free of egocentricity. If Saul had

2. Emily Bronte, *Wuthering Heights*, edited by David Daiches. Baltimore: Penguin Books, 1961, p. 120.

learned from this experience, the course of his later life might still have been changed, but unfortunately Saul soon forgot David's love for him and only remembered his former fears. As Kunkel once said, "We always forget the lessons of life which could help us to overcome our egocentricity. In this respect we are almost morons. But we remember well what suits our Ego; there we are ingenious and alert."[3]

David instinctively knows this. He does not trust Saul's promises and reassurances and returns to the wilderness. Soon Saul is pursuing him again and once more David has to flee. This time David realizes he can no longer stay in Israel, and after he says farewell to his friend Jonathan he seeks sanctuary in the land of the Philistines. The Philistine King Achish is naturally suspicious of David, but David pleads that he is an exile and assures Achish that he will be a good vassal to him. Achish sees that David is an outlaw and allows him to stay in the land, but he keeps a close eye on him. In order to convince Achish of his loyalty to him David tells him that he is going to raid the Israelites and bring back the booty. He does go on numerous raids and brings treasures back to the Philistines, but he raids the Amalekites and other common enemies and doesn't raid his own people. The deception works, and Achish trusts David and allows him to remain.

At this point we are told:

Samuel died, and the whole of Israel assembled to mourn him. They buried him at his home in Ramah (1 Samuel 25:1)

According to ancient Hebrew belief, when a person died he went to Sheol. In Sheol his former personality continued to live but as a *rephaim*—a mere shade of his former self. Those

3. Fritz Kunkel, *Creation Continues*, original edition, 1952, p. 214.

who lived in Sheol existed in a dim and shadowy world with no further relationship to Yahweh, who was God only for the living. In Sheol there was neither reward for the righteous nor punishment for the wicked; there was no pain, but neither was there hope. Except under special circumstances the departed no longer had contact with the world of the living. Samuel, therefore, passes out of our story—until the very end.

The stage is now set for the final act of our drama. Saul is still king, but is oppressed by his dark fears; David, who might have been his helper, has been driven into exile with the Philistines; Samuel is now in Sheol and can no longer intervene for better or worse in the fortunes of Israel. And Israel itself is threatened by the resurgent power of its most feared enemy, the Philistines.

7

Transformation

Forces now converge on the unfortunate Saul that bring a fate that is inevitable. The Philistines, sensing the weakness of their enemy, invade the land of Israel again, but the greatest enemy of Saul is within himself: his deep fears. Against these he is helpless, and they now suck from him his courage, resourcefulness, and manhood. The more desperately he tries to defend his ego against these inner enemies, the more he is in the grip of them. In desperation Saul tries again to find guidance from Yahweh. Our text tells us:

> Meanwhile the Philistines had mustered and pitched camp at Shunem. Saul mustered all Israel and they encamped at Gilboa. When Saul saw the Philistine camp he was afraid and there was a great trembling in his heart. Saul consulted Yahweh, but Yahweh gave him no answer, either by dream or oracle or prophet (1 Samuel 28:4–7).

The Philistine host is awesome. It would have been even more awesome if David had been part of it. In fact, David had been urged by King Achish to join him in the fight against Israel; he dared not openly refuse for then he would be suspected of treason. Achish said to him:

'It is understood that you join forces with me, you and your men?'

David answered with a subtle ambiguity that escaped the notice of the king:

'In that case, you will soon see what your servant can do' (1 Samuel 28:1–2).

So David is forced to assemble his men along with the Philistines. We don't know what David would have done if he had been ordered to march with the army when it went to war, but fortunately he is let off the hook, for the other Philistine generals object. No doubt they remember the Hebrew troops who defected in the midst of the battle when Jonathan charged the outpost and spread panic throughout the army. They say to their king:

'Is not this the David of whom they sang in the dance:

"Saul has killed his thousands,
David his tens of thousands?" ' (1 Samuel 29:5).

So Achish is forced to tell David that he must remain behind. David feigns disappointment, but of course he is greatly relieved.

If David had been thinking only of himself he might have welcomed the chance to march with the Philistines. He could have taken revenge on Saul, and with Philistine power behind him, he could have become the king himself. The Real Self emerges in David again. He is above the desire for personal vengeance, and too much at one with his people to put his own ambitions ahead of their welfare. David acts from "We" and not from "I."

But Saul is wholly engrossed in his personal survival, and, as we have seen, is so desperate that for the first time since he performed the sacrifice at Gilgal he tries to make a relationship with Yahweh. The methods that he uses are instructive: dream, oracle, and prophet.

We are familiar with the use of oracle. It was the casting of the sacred lots that would answer a question "yea" or "nay" but might, on rare occasions, give no answer at all. When the latter happened it meant that the questioner had been cut off from Yahweh. When Saul received no answer from the oracle it reinforced his fear that he was now truly rejected.

We know from other places in the Old Testament that dreams were revered by the ancient Hebrews as one way Yahweh spoke to humankind. It is especially significant to note that Yahweh used dreams to speak to an individual person about his destiny. This is a departure from the usual Hebrew attitude that portrayed Yahweh as only interested in Israel as a whole. Yahweh spoke to Jacob, for instance, when he fled into the desert from Esau's wrath. He sent dreams repeatedly to Joseph, and used a dream to guide Gideon to victory over the Midianites. But Saul had no dreams.

There are many reasons people do not remember their dreams.[1] We are not told why Saul was unable to recall them but it is possible that he fell prey to what might be called "the disparaging voice." It often happens that people who say they don't recall their dreams actually are remembering them, but

---

1. For a more complete discussion of why some people do not remember their dreams, see pages 12–14 of my book *Dreams and Healing*.

when they start to write them down a poisonous thought goes through their minds saying something like, "Oh don't bother with that; it's only a fragment; it's not important; it's not really a dream." Instead of challenging this thought some people succumb to it and then are convinced that they are not dreaming. In fact, it sometimes happens that when we start to record what appears to be a dream fragment the whole dream is recalled. It's like catching hold of one end of a tiger's tail—one soon discovers there is a tiger at the other end of it.

Also there were prophets. The kind of prophets the text refers to were certain ecstatics whose ability to go into a trance-like state was taken as a sign of their closeness to the divine world. Such supposedly inspired people might be consulted in times of crisis; it was thought that they might have access to guidance that ordinary people didn't have. But evidently the prophets couldn't help Saul either.

It's interesting to note that prayer is not mentioned. Prayer rests upon the idea that the individual can have personal fellowship with God. Examples of individuals praying to Yahweh are relatively scarce in the Old Testament, perhaps because Yahweh was a dangerous, awe-inspiring deity whom only the specially courageous and gifted might dare approach. (Moses, e.g., talks with Yahweh on Mt. Sinai but the people as a whole want nothing to do with him.) Perhaps for this reason it doesn't occur to Saul to pray, although this is, perhaps, exactly what he should have done. Prayer alone might have given Saul a chance to confess his egocentricity to himself and to his Creator and find an opportunity for release.

Can an egocentric prayer do any good? An interesting example is found in the story of King Claudius' prayer in Shakespeare's *Hamlet* (Act III, Scene 3). Claudius was a thoroughly egocentric man. He had murdered his brother and married his brother's wife in order to achieve his selfish ambitions. But he has a guilty conscience, and fears divine punishment. In this spirit he turns to prayer after asking himself,

> What form of prayer
> can serve my turn?

His prayer is clearly not an attempt to relate to God's will, but to get God to salvage him from the consequences of his actions. Claudius doesn't want to change, he only wants protection from divine justice. For this reason his prayer is not answered. Nevertheless two important things happened to Claudius while he prayed. First, he gained insight into just how egocentric he was:

> Help, angels! Make assay.
> Bow, stubborn knees; and, heart with strings of steel,
> Be soft as sinews of the new-born babe!
> All may be well.

And after his prayer is finished he rises to his feet with the realization:

> My words fly up, my thoughts remain below:
> Words without thoughts never to heaven go.

Second, although he did not know it, his prayer saved him from being murdered. While he was praying Hamlet stole up behind him intending to kill him. But when Hamlet saw him in prayer he changed his mind because he feared that if Claudius died while he was praying his soul would go to heaven:

> Now might I do it pat, now he is praying;
> And now I'll do't. And so he goes to heaven;

And so am I reveng'd. That would be scann'd:
A villain kills my father; and for that,
I, his sole son, do this same villain send
To heaven.
Why, this is hire and salary, not revenge.

If Saul had prayed he might have had an experience like that of Claudius. It would have seemed as though God made no reply, yet small but significant changes might have taken place in him. But it was not in the collective spirit of his age for him to pray, and though Saul's destiny is to reach beyond the collective spirit for his own relationship with Yahweh, he is not up to that spiritual task. So he does not pray, and his unconscious does not yield to his attempts to find guidance because his motives are too egocentric.

When we approach the unconscious it is important to do so in the right spirit. In the story of Joseph, to which we have already alluded, there is an example of this. Joseph is in Pharaoh's dungeon when he is joined by Pharaoh's cup-bearer and baker, who have fallen into disfavor with Pharaoh and have been imprisoned. One day Joseph notices that they are looking even more depressed than usual and asks them what troubles them. They reply,

'We have had a dream, but there is no one to interpret it'
(Genesis 40:8)

Joseph replies significantly,

'Are not interpretations God's business? Come, tell me.'

Then the cup-bearer tells Joseph his dream, and Joseph gives him a favorable interpretation: in three days Pharaoh will bring the cup-bearer out of the dungeon and restore him to his former position in the court. Then we are told:

The chief baker, seeing that the interpretation had been favourable, said to Joseph, 'I too had a dream.'

He goes on to tell his dream, but Joseph's interpretation is that in three days Pharaoh will have the baker executed. And so it turned out; the cup-bearer was restored to the court, and the baker was killed.

The difference between the cup-bearer and the baker is that the cup-bearer risked himself with his dream. He asked for an interpretation without knowing whether it would be to his liking or not. In this way he put his ego on the line and took his chances with his dream. Such a positive attitude made an ally of his unconscious. The baker, however, approached his dream egocentrically; he risked an interpretation only when he felt sure that it would be what he wanted to hear. It was because he had the wrong attitude that the inner powers turned against him.

Saul seeks divine guidance with the attitude of the baker and of King Claudius. He doesn't want the truth, but is thrashing around for a way to save himself. Therefore he gets no help.

Much the same thing can happen in modern analysis or spiritual direction. When most people seek help they are motivated by more or less egocentric reasons. We want to be free of some pain or difficulty, and if analysis and working with our dreams can help us rid ourselves of our uncomfortable situation, we'll try it. But we can also be motivated by a desire to find out about the truth of our situation. Our attitude can be, "Okay, I'm desperate. I've got to do something. If a dream might help I'll take a chance with it." However, if we approach analysis with the exclusively egocentric attitude that the baker displayed we can expect little to come of our psychological work.

Saul is now so desperate that he turns for help to a strange source: a necromancer. Necromancers claimed the ability to enter into a trance and conjure up the appearance of a shade from Sheol. They were anathema to Yahweh, and were repeatedly denounced in the Old Testament. The Deuteronomic Law condemned anyone who was ". . . an enchanter, or a witch, or a charmer, or a consulter with familiar spirits, or a wizard, or a necromancer" (Deuteronomy 18:10–11 KJV). It's not clear whether necromancy was taken over by the Hebrews from the Canaanites and their worship of Astarte, or whether it was always part of the Hebrew "underground" religion. In any case, Saul, once a zealous defender of Yahweh, had tried to extirpate necromancy in the land. Now, however, he is driven in his extremity to say to his servants:

> 'Find a woman who is a necromancer for me to go and consult her.' His servants replied, 'There is a necromancer at En-dor' (1 Samuel 28:7).

It's interesting that Saul's servants seem to know right away where a necromancer could be found. Evidently in spite of Saul's efforts to eliminate them some of them survived and were still frequented by people who were otherwise Yahweh's devotees. It is virtually impossible to completely eradicate an opposing religious belief as long as that belief has inner vitality; there is always someone here or there who survives the persecution and carries on the old faith in secret.

When a belief survives it is for a psychological reason; the unconscious sees to it that every belief survives that still has psychological validity. The ego adopts and refines a conscious system of belief about God. But no conscious belief system is complete. Each one is bound to be in error or deficiency in some way. This means that somewhere within us, no matter what our conscious religious (or political) belief, there is a doubt and contradiction. Certain people are "selected" by the collective unconscious to espouse the rejected or overlooked point of view and keep it alive in the world. So the world is divided between Catholics and Protestants, Christians and Jews, Western religious beliefs and Eastern ones, because all of them have a certain validity and none of them is exclusively correct.

The scene that follows is worthy of Shakespeare. In true storytelling fashion we are only told what is necessary and our imagination fills in the gaps:

> And so Saul, disguising himself and changing his clothes, set out accompanied by two men; their visit to the woman took place at night. 'Disclose the future to me' he said 'by means of a ghost. Conjure up the one I shall name to you.' The woman answered, 'Look, you know what Saul has done, how he has swept the necromancers and wizards out of the country; why are you setting a trap for my life, then, to have me killed?' But Saul swore to her by Yahweh, 'As Yahweh lives,' he said 'no blame shall attach to you for this business.' Then the woman asked, 'Whom shall I conjure up for you?' He replied, 'Conjure up Samuel' (1 Samuel 28:8–11).

Now we know why Saul wants to meet with the necromancer: he wants to talk with Samuel. Cut off from Yahweh, he desperately hopes that perhaps Samuel will have some word for him that might give him hope or encouragement. The story continues:

> Then the woman saw Samuel and, giving a great cry, she said to Saul, 'Why have you deceived me? You are Saul.' The king said, 'Do not be afraid! What do you see?' The woman answered Saul, 'I see a ghost rising up from the earth.' 'What is he like?' he asked. She answered, 'It is an old man coming up; he is wrapped in a cloak.' Then Saul knew it was Samuel and he bowed down his face to the ground and did homage (1 Samuel 28:12–14).

Samuel looms up as a gaunt and forbidding old man, a ghastly shade from Sheol. The opening of the talk between the two men is not auspicious for Saul. Samuel says to him:

> 'Why have you disturbed my rest, conjuring me up?' Saul replied, 'I am in great distress; the Philistines are waging war against me, and God has abandoned me and no longer answers me either by prophet or dream; and so I have summoned you to tell me what I must do.'

It is a pitiful plea for help, and one would think it might melt even Samuel's steely heart. But Samuel has no pity in him:

> 'And why do you consult me, when Yahweh has abandoned you and is with your neighbour? Yahweh has done to you as he foretold through me; he has snatched the sovereignty from your hand and given it to your neighbour, David. . . . That is why Yahweh treats you like this now. What is more, Yahweh will deliver Israel and you, too, into the power of the Philistines. Tomorrow you and your sons will be with me; and Israel's army, too, for Yahweh will deliver it into the power of the Philistines' (1 Samuel 28:15–19).

Samuel remained a Nero even in Sheol; he still relishes the power he has over Saul. He apparently enjoys seeing Saul crushed like a worm, and pronounces judgment upon his victim without qualm or compassion. Even if Samuel sincerely believed Saul's situation was hopeless he might have added some word of spiritual encouragement. But apparently it's not enough for Samuel that Saul should die—he must also be completely crushed.

And Saul is crushed. After Samuel's dreadful pronouncement he loses whatever remnant of courage he had and falls into total despair. In the face of his inexorable fate the man comes completely unglued. The once seemingly mighty Nero collapses and becomes a craven Turtle:

> Saul was overcome and fell full-length on the ground. He was terrified by what Samuel had said, and, besides this, he was weakened by having eaten nothing at all that day and all that night.

But at last help comes—and from an unexpected direction: the much maligned necromancer, a woman who was once persecuted by this helpless hulk of a man who lies prostrate on the floor of the cave. A few months earlier Saul would have gladly cut off her head if he could have caught her, yet it is she, not Samuel, who has compassion for the hapless Saul. But she has more than compassion: she also perceives that Saul is, in spite of everything, a royal personality who should not, and need not, be groveling on the ground. She sees Saul as God saw him from the beginning, and acts now to bring him out of his craven condition:

> The woman then came to Saul, and seeing his terror said, 'Look, your servant has obeyed your voice; I have taken my life in my hands, and have obeyed the command you gave me. So now you in your turn listen to what your servant says. Let me set a little food before you for you to eat and get some strength for your journey.' But he refused. 'I will not eat' he said. His servants however pressed him, and so did the woman. Allowing himself to be persuaded by them, he rose from the ground and sat on the divan. The woman owned a fattened calf which she quickly

slaughtered, and she took some flour and kneaded it and with it baked cakes of unleavened bread; she put these before Saul and his servants; and after they had eaten they set off and left the same night (1 Samuel 28:20–25).

Samuel was wrong after all. Saul wasn't entirely cut off from God, for God acted through this woman to restore Saul to himself. It is true that it is too late for Saul to save his throne, or even his life, but it wasn't too late for Saul to save his soul.

God acting through the necromancer? The thought must surely offend Jew and Christian alike. In fact, it is so unlikely that it seems to have escaped the attention of commentators for centuries that it was this persecuted woman who ministered to the stricken king. Yet in the Bible God repeatedly confounds human reason and expectations. The aged Sarah just laughed when God told her that she, who no longer even menstruated, would have a child. It certainly never occurred to Joseph when he was sold as a slave in Egypt that everything that was happening was part of God's plan. Moses was startled almost beyond belief to find himself talking with God in the burning bush. The prophet Hosea shocked the people of Israel by comparing God's relationship with them with his relationship with the harlot Gomer. And who would have thought that God would act to save humankind by being born into the world as a helpless child? Certainly not the innkeeper who turned Mary and Joseph aside, nor the disciples who were convinced that when Jesus died on the cross it was the end of everything.

We decide how things have to be done, but God is full of surprises, and the individuation process is made up of unexpected twists and turns. At the moment we are convinced that we have all the answers, we are in the greatest danger of losing the way. At the moment we think we are in possession of the truth, we are most likely to be ignorant, for at that moment we will stop looking for it. It's better to be like a woodsman following a faint trail in the wilderness, uncertain, eyes open and alert because he never knows which way that trail will suddenly turn.

Saul, strengthened physically and spiritually, goes to meet his fate. He will die, but now he will die like a man—on his feet, living his life to the end, and dying as a hero and a king should die. At last he does what he should have done much earlier: he embraces the darkness and goes *through* his crisis. Going through his crisis at this time means going to meet death. In this way he gives up trying to save his precious ego, but in surrendering it he meets the Self.

Saul could have gone through his crisis earlier. For instance, when Samuel made his awful pronouncement and Saul was tormented by his dark fears, he might have said to himself: "All right, perhaps Yahweh has rejected me. Perhaps I am unworthy to be king and another man is already chosen to take my place. If this is the will of Yahweh, I will accept it. His will is superior to mine and I will therefore consent to giving up my throne and even my life whenever God calls for it. In the meantime I am still the king, and I will be the king as fearlessly and skillfully as I can as long as I am allowed to do so. My prayer will be that I will be helped by Yahweh to be a good king during the time that remains to me, and if Yahweh should relent, and allow me to keep my throne, then so be it."

Such an attitude would have amounted to a voluntary surrender of the ego, the "mortification" of the ego and the dissolution of his egocentricity. With such an attitude he would no longer have tried to save himself, and would have found what truly supports him: the Self within. Free of fear, because he no longer had anything to protect, Saul's creative energies would have been released. The words of Jesus come to mind:

For what is a man profited, if he shall gain the whole world, and lose his own soul? (Matthew 16:26 KJV).

and

He that loseth his life for my sake shall find it (Matthew 10:39 KJV).

More than that, he would have realized that the very experiences he dreaded the most contained the most saving grace. As Kunkel put it:

No one can voluntarily decrease his egocentricity or idolatry. The only thing we can do, and the only useful interpretation of the central Christian imperative is: do not run away from your crises; try to stand the impact of reality and to discover the light behind darkness; do not resist evil. Then evil will be found to be grace.[2]

Could Saul have changed his fate if he had embraced his crisis this way? A good question, but it comes from the old egocentric ego, still looking for a way out. The darkness must be entered into with no conditions. We can pray, but the best prayer will be for the strength or courage or whatever quality it takes to see the experience through to the end. As soon as we try to place conditions on our acceptance of the experience the old ego creeps back in. Like the cup-bearer in Pharaoh's dungeon who risked himself with his dream, we have to risk ourselves come what may. Naturally we will hope things may turn out for the best, but our egocentricity will die only if we are willing to accept whatever may come.

---

2. *Fritz Kunkel: Selected Writings.* New York: Paulist Press, 1984, p. 268.

The crisis may come upon us as an outer event or an inner event or both. If it is an inner event it involves a recognition of something about ourselves that seems unacceptable—yet must be accepted. Jungian analyst David Hart points out the necessity of "facing the unacceptable." Although he doesn't use the term egocentricity it is clear from the following passage that this is what he is referring to:

> Many people fear that if they face the unacceptable, they will become it. The exact reverse is true. If you do not face it, you become it. It will always be lived out in one way or another. . . . The turning point comes when something in us decides that the unacceptable is really meant for us, and we begin to look for its meaning. Then there is an experience of it while we remain also separate from it, and this combination is the essential one for real integration.
>
> If, on the other hand, we employ our usual means not to face what is meant for us—and each of us has his own particular escapes—the terror of the unacceptable not only remains within us, but is also always being lived out as a real disturbance in our lives. We then need constant reassurance that 'it is not really so,' a precarious and unreal base on which to live.[3]

On the other hand, the unacceptable may also be an outer event: some calamity, an illness, a death, a shameful event that cannot be avoided, but must somehow be accepted as Christ accepted the cross. Going through such a crisis means bearing the unbearable.

Our text continues:

> The Philistines made war on Israel and the men of Israel fled from the Philistines and were slaughtered on Mount

---

3. From an article "The Path to Wholeness" in *Psychological Perspectives*, Fall, 1972, p. 152.

Gilboa. The Philistines pressed Saul and his sons hard and killed Jonathan, Abinadab and Malchishua, the sons of Saul. The fighting grew heavy about Saul; the bowmen took him off his guard, so that he fell wounded by the bowmen. Then Saul said to his armour-bearer, 'Draw your sword and run me through with it; I do not want these uncircumcised men to come and gloat over me.' But his armour-bearer was afraid and would not do it. So Saul took his own sword and fell on it. His armour-bearer, seeing that Saul was dead, fell on his sword too and died with him. And so Saul and his three sons and his armour-bearer died together that day. When the Israelites who were on the other side of the valley saw that the men of Israel had taken flight and that Saul and his sons were dead, they abandoned their towns and fled. The Philistines then came and occupied them (1 Samuel 31:1–7).

At the end of his life Saul gave up his ego, faced the unacceptable, and embraced his inevitable death; in so doing he became his true Self at last. But now we read that he killed himself. We have to come to terms with Saul's apparent suicide.

There is only one clear example of suicide in the Old Testament, found in Chapter 17 of 2 Samuel. David's son Absalom has rebelled against his father and usurped the throne. Absalom's chief advisor is the wily Ahithophel, but one of David's friends, Hushai, has come to Absalom's court and persuaded Absalom that he is loyal to him. Absalom asks advice from both Ahithophel and Hushai regarding how he should proceed in the war against David. Ahithophel says he should attack at once before David can organize an army; Hushai argues that Absalom should wait. Hushai's advice is accepted, and when Ahithophel sees that, he knows this means David will win. Rather than face the consequences he goes home and strangles himself.

Other apparent suicides are found in Judges 9:54ff, 1 Kings 16:19ff, and in the story of Samson. But Samson's self-imposed death is not a genuine suicide. He pulled the Temple of Dagon down upon himself but did so in order to kill the Philistines and show the power of Yahweh. Samson doesn't kill himself in order to escape something painful, but to fulfill his purpose.

It is the same with Saul. He kills himself because, under the circumstances, it was the only honorable thing to do. If he had stayed alive to save his own skin and eke out a few more miserable weeks of life, it would have meant disgrace for himself, his people, and Yahweh.

The Oriental ethic about taking your own life has always been different from the Western one, and Israel was Oriental in this respect. According to the Oriental view, it is shameful to allow yourself to fall into the hands of the enemy. If you allow yourself to be captured it is because you are a coward and afraid to die. If your cause is lost, and it is a choice between being captured or self-imposed death, you choose the latter. In World War II, for example, Japanese soldiers practically never surrendered. When they were defeated they chose death instead. Sometimes they killed each other, sometimes they made a suicidal charge into the face of the American machine guns. With few exceptions the only Japanese prisoners of war were soldiers too badly wounded to avoid capture. In fact, one reason the Japanese treated American prisoners of war so badly may have been because they scorned them for surrendering instead of dying.

This was Saul's moral code. If he allowed himself to be captured it would have been a terrible disgrace. What was the value of a few more weeks of life if it allowed the Philistines to mock Yahweh by holding up to scorn Israel's captured king? In fact, the Philistines did all they could to mock Saul as it was by refusing the body of Saul honorable burial and fastening it to the wall of one of their cities for everyone to deride:

> When the Philistines came on the following day to strip the dead, they found Saul and his three sons lying on Mount Gilboa. They cut off his head and, stripping him of his armour, had it carried round the land of the Philistines to proclaim the good news to their idols and their people. They placed his armour in the temple of Astarte; they fastened his body to the wall of Beth-shan (1 Samuel 31:9–10).

So Saul dies, and the victory of the Philistines is complete, but the story is not quite over for we have not yet reckoned with the people of Jabesh-gilead. It will be remembered that Saul, in his first kingly act, rescued the people of Jabesh-gilead from the Ammonites, and the people were enormously grateful to him. Now they prove their love and loyalty for their slain benefactor by risking their lives to rescue his desecrated body:

> When the inhabitants of Jabesh-gilead heard what the Philistines had done to Saul, all the warriors set out, marching throughout the night, and took the bodies of Saul and his sons off the wall of Beth-shan, and bringing them to Jabesh they burned them there. Then they took their bones and buried them under the tamarisk of Jabesh, and fasted for seven days (1 Samuel 31:11–13).

Saul is dead. Was he a madman? Was he, as Samuel kept saying, a disobedient and evil person whom Yahweh rightly rejected? Or was he a man who made many mistakes, and in so doing taught us a great deal, but who in the end pointed the way to wholeness? I have argued that Saul was called to individuation, took a step in that direction, then fled from the call

and almost destroyed himself in the process, but in the end
embraced death and found his true Self again. It is not where
you are in the middle of the race that counts, but where you
are at the end. Now I must leave it to others to judge the man
and the rightness of my appeal for him. But we are three thousand years away. How can we know? How can we judge him
correctly? We are likely to be blinded to his reality by our
biases. The conservatives among us may choose to believe
Samuel's estimate. The rebels, if that's what we are, may favor
Saul in spite of everything. But there is one person who arrived at a judgment about Saul who was close to him, someone
uniquely qualified to know the man as only God could know
him. He was a man with every reason to judge him negatively,
a man who had just cause to hate him. Yet he did not, but
loved him to the end: David. When word is brought to David
that the Israelites have been defeated on Mount Gilboa, and
that Jonathan and Saul are dead, David sings a song of lament.
With David's lament I rest my case for Saul:

> Alas, the glory of Israel has been slain on your heights!
> How did the heroes fall?
>
> Do not speak of it in Gath,
> nor announce it in the streets of Ashkelon,
> or the daughters of the Philistines will rejoice,
> the daughters of the uncircumcised will gloat.
>
> O mountains of Gilboa,
> let there be no dew or rain on you;
> treacherous fields,
> for there the hero's shield was dishonoured!
>
> The shield of Saul was anointed not with oil
> but with blood of the wounded, fat of the warriors;
> the bow of Jonathan did not turn back,
> nor the sword of Saul return idle.

Saul and Jonathan, loved and lovely,
neither in life, nor in death, were divided.
Swifter than eagles were they,
stronger were they than lions.

O daughters of Israel, weep for Saul
who clothed you in scarlet and fine linen,
who set brooches of gold
on your garments.

How did the heroes fall
in the thick of the battle?

O Jonathan, in your death I am stricken,
I am desolate for you, Jonathan my brother.
Very dear to me you were,
your love to me more wonderful
than the love of a woman.

How did the heroes fall
and the battle armour fail? (2 Samuel 1:19–27).

Appendix A
Depth Psychology Looks at Saul

The most important idea of C.G. Jung for our purposes is his concept of *individuation*. Individuation is the name Jung gave to the lifelong process that goes on within us that seeks to bring about the development of a whole personality. Individuation is not something we consciously decide to do, but is a necessity thrust upon us from within. Jung calls the urge to individuate or become whole our most important and central instinct, and believed it is the psychological basis for our religious urges and ideas.

The individuation process revolves around the relationship between the ego and the Self. The ego is the "I" part of us. It has been called the "executive of the conscious personality." It is the part of us with which we are most closely identified; in fact most people suppose that their personality doesn't go any farther than the boundaries of the ego even though, in fact, the much larger part of us is contained in the unconscious.

The Self is the name Jung gave to the whole person. The Self can be thought of as our genuine, authentic, and complete personality. The Self embraces both conscious and unconscious in a paradoxical totality. It exists within us from the beginning as a potentiality and as the source of our future creative development, but if individuation is to take place the vital life of the Self must be realized through the life that we actually live. For this the "cooperation" of the ego is necessary, for the ego is to become like a vessel through which the Self is fulfilled and expressed.

It can be said that everything that lives seeks to individuate because every living thing has its proper goal. For instance, when we look at a great oak tree we could say that there is an acorn that has individuated. Individuation, therefore, is as common and ordinary as life, and yet, of course, it is a most marvelous and wonderful event when some unit of life does indeed fulfill the purpose for which it was intended.

The idea of individuation is crucial to Jung's understanding of illness and health. When individuation takes place the ego is healthy and vital, but when individuation is thwarted or denied, neurotic symptoms, boredom, and other manifestations of illness appear.

If individuation is to take place there must be a relationship between the ego and the Self. Now if two nations want to have a relationship they exchange ambassadors who go back and forth between them. Similarly, it's important for the ego and the Self to have a way to communicate with each other. Functionally, prayer is one of the many ways the ego reaches out to the Self. Dreams can be understood as an important way that the Self reaches out to the ego. When there is a living connection between the two we speak of the "ego-Self axis" and individuation then becomes possible, but when this axis is non-existent or defective, psychological and spiritual development does not take place in the proper way.

For individuation to occur, the ego must develop a certain kind of awareness, and live an authentic life. This is why Jung's psychology stresses the importance of becoming psychologically conscious. However, people individuate without the benefit of formal psychology. Wherever people become genuine, and grow as individuals, individuation takes place.

For all practical purposes an experience with the Self is

like an experience with God. While Jung does not exactly equate God and Self he does say that the Self is like a vessel filled with the divine grace. This is why, psychologically speaking, the figure of Yahweh in the Old Testament can be taken as a symbol of the Self. It was the genius of the Hebrews to develop first monolatry and then monotheism. This paved the way for a greater relationship between ego and Self. This is why we will find that the relationship between Samuel and Saul on the one hand and Yahweh on the other hand is so important for our psychological understanding of the story.

The process of becoming psychologically conscious includes an awareness of our shadow personality. The "shadow" is the name Jung gave to the dark, unwanted side of our personality. It is "that part of the personality which has been repressed for the sake of the ego ideal."[1] In short, those qualities that might have been incorporated into the ego but were rejected because they were feared, or deemed unworthy or immoral, drop into the unconscious and form a secondary personality within us known as the shadow. Because we are ordinarily unaware of the shadow it lives an autonomous unconscious existence—playing out the Mr. Hyde to our Dr. Jekyll.

Since the shadow includes those qualities that have been rejected, its nature, aims, goals, and actions are counter to our conscious nature and goals. Of course this means that our personality becomes divided. It is important to recognize and make a relationship with our shadow in order that this split in us be healed; otherwise we can't be whole people.

Becoming whole also calls for the recognition of our contra-sexual side. A man is not entirely masculine; he has a feminine side as well. And a woman is not entirely feminine; she

---

1. Edward C. Whitmont, *The Symbolic Quest.* Princeton University Press, 1969, p. 160.

has a masculine side too. Since the ego of a man is ordinarily identified with his masculinity, his feminine side appears in the unconscious and is called by Jung the *anima*. Conversely, in a woman, whose ego identification is feminine, her masculine side functions unconsciously and is known as the *animus*.

The Self, shadow, anima and animus are basic psychological patterns in the personalities of all of us. Jung called these basic psychological patterns within us *archetypes*. They are contained in the *collective unconscious*, the name Jung gave to the archetypal structure of the human psyche that is common to us all. Jung distinguished the collective unconscious from the personal unconscious, which contains the repressed or forgotten experiences and emotions that are peculiar to a given individual and are the result of that person's particular life experiences.

The collective unconscious expresses itself through symbols. These symbols appear in dreams, fantasies, myths, fairy tales—anyplace where the unconscious spontaneously represents itself. Jung has shown that the symbols of the collective unconscious represent and help relate us to the individuation process. Therefore, a study of these symbols produced by the unconscious can help us understand the nature of the Self and the process of becoming whole.

The process of individuation takes a lifetime of give-and-take between conscious and unconscious, ego and Self, man and God. It's possible to make general statements about this process, as I am doing here, but how it actually takes place in a particular person can't be predicted or determined in advance. Because each of us is a unique person, our process of individuation will also be unique. Individuation therefore requires what we might call the discovery of our personal and unique path through life. Each person must find and learn her own individual path; the way cannot be learned by collective means. For this reason, while general religous and psychological instructions may be helpful, they are no substitute for the uncertainties of the individual journey, any more than a map takes the place of actually undertaking a trip through a strange country.

As mentioned before, although modern psychology can be extremely helpful, people individuate by living life faithfully and completely and learning from their relationships and experiences. People individuated long before Jung came on the scene to describe the process scientifically. In fact, I argue in my book, *The Man Who Wrestled With God*, that the oldest extant "case histories" of individuation are found in the stories of Jacob, Joseph and Moses in the Book of Genesis. To these stories must be added the story of Saul, though whether or not he succeeded in his individuation is the matter we have to determine.

In the Introduction I spoke of the hero. From the psychological point of view individuation is a heroic process. In fact, to become whole does require heroic efforts from us. All the qualities of the hero—courage, resourcefulness, resilience, the spirit of self-sacrifice, and psychological honesty—are required of the person who becomes whole. A hero is not only a person whose outer achievements win renown and respect. He or she may also be a person who wins an inner struggle, even though no one else knows that the struggle and the victory have taken place.

While Jung said a great many important things about individuation, another psychologist, Fritz Kunkel, fills in a few gaps in Jung's picture. As we have seen, for individuation to take place the Self must be realized and expressed through the ego. This living relationship and mutual dependence of ego and Self can be likened to a bottle of wine. In a bottle of wine, the wine is the important element, but if the wine is to be used it must flow out through the neck of the bottle. When the ego is functioning as it is meant to, it is related to the Self as the neck of a bottle is to the wine: it becomes the organ of the psyche through which the vital life of the Self emerges. However, sometimes we refer to something as a "bottleneck"; this means that something is obstructing a flow rather than assisting it. When the ego is too narrow and constricted it is like such a bottleneck because it impedes the expression of the Self. Kunkel called such a condition "egocentricity." When the ego is egocentric, individuation is thwarted and creative development becomes impossible. Kunkel's most important contribution to psychology is his study of the origin, nature, and effects of egocentricity, and the life crisis that it takes to rid us of our egocentricity so the genuine life in us can emerge. In order to see more clearly what Kunkel meant we will need to look at Kunkel's view of the genuine life that comes from the Self, and the false life of the egocentric ego.

The Self, Kunkel felt, was a positive, creative force. An experience of the Self gives us vitality, courage, creativity, and energy, and also connects us meaningfully to other people. When the Self is constellated in a relationship, the subject is no longer "I" but "We," that is, ego-identity gives way to Self-identity, and Self-identity includes others. From this comes the capacity to love, the ability to sacrifice oneself for others, and the ability to lead others for their benefit and not for our own egocentric gratification.

Kunkel saw the parallel between his psychological ideas and Christian theological ideas about the nature of our relationship to God. The Self is the creative energy and purpose of the Creator manifested within us; for this reason, to live from the Self as our Center is to live in accordance with God's will. Sin, on the other hand, is the egocentric deviation of the ego from the Self.

To live from the Self does not necessarily mean that we will be happy. To the contrary, living from the Self may bring us into conflict with our culture and with other people around us. The "pursuit of happiness" is the goal of the ego, not of the Self. But a life from the Self will be a creative life, and no matter how bad things may become the Self will enable us to have a vital and creative response. In the long run, only this kind of life is truly satisfying.

Unfortunately, instead of letting the Self be the Center, the ego tries to be the Center. When this happens we speak of "egocentricity." To say the ego is egocentric means that it is interested only in its own defense and the fulfillment of its own ambitions. When we are in this defensive and ego-centered state, the creative life of the Self is blocked, and a distortion enters into our personality that breeds evil. Kunkel believed that all of us are thrust into a defensive, life-negating egocentric posture because of destructive influences on the naturally trusting child from egocentric parents and other significant adults. The natural "we" of the child becomes the defensive "I" of the ego. Thus egocentricity creates more egocentricity.

Life within the egocentric ego is like living in a heavily defended castle. As long as our castle appears to be well defended we feel secure. We fail to realize that as long as we are confined to our castle we might as well be in prison. For in contrast to the free and creative life of the Real Self, the life of the egocentric ego is rigid, narrow, and fearful. But if we have never experienced the Self we don't know the difference between the two states of mind.

Our egocentricity can be blatant and obvious, at least to everyone else, or extremely subtle. The ego is a great cheat, and, if clever enough, is capable of posing successfully as a saint when in fact a great deception is in progress. The ego, of course, has a great resistance to seeing its own egocentricity, for while such insight would not by itself free us from our egocentricity it would make us uncomfortable with it and would be a harbinger of its eventual destruction. This we fear because we don't believe that we could survive without our castle. We suppose nothing will hold us up if we surrender our egocentricity; we are like a person who clings frantically to a drifting log in the sea because he doesn't know that if he only lets go he could swim to shore. Yet the more the ego resists surrendering itself, the more alienated it becomes from the Self. Since the Self is the source of love, strength, and energy, the result of this alienation is loneliness, anxiety, and depression.

We are lonely when we cannot express how we feel to other people. Egocentricity distorts both the inner and outer situation in such a way that loneliness is a result. To the extent we are egocentric we cannot express how we feel because a genuine expression of feeling makes us vulnerable, and this must be resisted at all costs. Further, to the extent we are egocentric we will alienate other people, so the loss of human relationship is the inevitable result of our egocentricity. Egocentric people are a drain on the energy of others, being unbearably inflated, tyrannical, or boring, so egocentricity drives others away. (The only exception is the apparent camaraderie of egocentric people who become allies with each other because there is a secret agreement to mutually support each other's egocentricity. Kunkel called such a group "the associated egos.") But we will also be lonely because in our egocentric state we are cut off from what Toronto analyst Daryl Sharp called "inner companions." A person in touch with the Real Self is not lonely even when by herself because of the great wealth of inner thoughts, imaginative ideas, and sudden inspirations that come up from within. But when we lack this connection to the dynamic center, our consciousness is like a barren desert on which nothing can grow.

When the Self tries to break through our egocentric defenses we experience anxiety. Anxiety is like living in a castle when the enemy is battering away at the gate with a battering ram. (Fear comes from confrontation with an outer enemy; anxiety from an inner enemy.) The Self, of course, need not be our enemy; it only looks and acts like our enemy as long as it is shut out and denied. Jung once said that anxiety is the result of something big trying to get into something small. The Self is big, and the egocentric ego is small. To alleviate the anxiety the ego must grow and become large enough to let the Self in.

The ego has little energy of its own; our conscious life is dependent on sources of energy from the unconscious for its existence. The situation is roughly analogous to an industrial nation with few natural resources that is dependent on a constant flow of raw materials from beyond its realm. But when we live egocentrically we are cut off from the Self, the source of energy. The result is a depression. Depression is the opposite of anxiety. When we are anxious the Self has approached the gate of the castle; when we are depressed the Self has moved far away. This is why Kunkel once said that when we experience anxiety the intensity of life is increased, but the scope has decreased. The intensity of the anxiety comes from the energy of the Self. In depression, on the other hand, the energy of the Self has receded. The two states may alternate—like high and low tide.

Two important emotions characteristic of egocentricity are rage and guilt. Rage is to be distinguished from healthy anger. When a situation becomes intolerable to the human spirit, genuine anger is a healthy response. Rage comes when our egocentricity is threatened. If someone finds our weak spot, or threatens to break through our defenses, a defensive rage may burst out.

It's important to distinguish the different kinds of guilt. There is genuine guilt. This comes from an offense against the Self. When we exceed our proper boundaries, or fail to live genuinely, we experience genuine guilt. This guilt we need to assume and carry consciously. It will be painful to do so, but will not cripple us or make us neurotic. To the contrary, by carrying the guilt that really belongs to us we will become strong because we will be less egocentric.

Then there is the guilt that we feel when our egocentric defenses are succeeding. The strange thing is that at the very moment when we have achieved our egocentric goals and ambitions we have a nagging guilty conscience about it. Somewhere within us we know that something is not right. Chances are we will quickly brush aside this troublesome feeling, but if we are courageous enough to stop and look at it we will begin to see where we have gone the wrong way.

Finally, there is false guilt. This comes from introjected collective ideas of what we should be like and should be doing. It's as though we carry within us an inner critic who continually judges us according to certain collective, false standards. False guilt feelings diminish our self-esteem and confidence, rob us of energy, and bring about depression. We are the victims of this false guilt, but if we do not resist it, or, worse yet, if we indulge ourselves in it, then it perpetuates our egocentricity. If we allow ourselves to languish in guilt that doesn't belong to us it doesn't lead us to modesty but keeps the egocentric ego alive. We are then subject to inflation: we are so important in our own eyes that we hold ourselves super-responsible for everything that is happening to ourselves and others.

Sooner or later our egocentricity no longer works for us. An egocentric adaptation to life may succeed temporarily, but life conspires against it and one day it will begin to fail. When this moment comes there occurs what Kunkel called the "ego crisis." We experience this as a dreadful time, the "abyss," the −100 (minus one hundred) of our life, and we avoid it as long as we can. The fact is, the ego crisis is a moment of truth when we are offered the opportunity to get out of our egocentric state and begin to live creatively.

The way out is to "die," and the way to die is to go *through* the crisis rather than try to avoid it. We need to embrace the very darkness that we fear and, as quoted earlier, "to face the unacceptable," as Jungian analyst David Hart once put it. In the words of Jesus we need to stop resisting the evil we fear and go to meet it even if it seems to threaten us with destruction. What will be destroyed is our egocentricity, and what will die is the egocentric ego. It is like carrying the cross—but beyond the crucifixion is the resurrection which, psychologically, is the new life the ego finds when it is creatively related to the Self.

Kunkel believed there were four basic egocentric types and gave them names that indicate the essential characteristic of each one: the Clinging Vine, the Star, the Turtle, and the Nero (or Tyrant).

The Clinging Vine, as the name indicates, is a person who clings to others for strength. As a vine clings to a tree for support, so Clinging Vine clings to others for support. This is because Clinging Vine cannot believe that he can stand on his own—and doesn't want to believe it. His life is dedicated to the egocentric goal of finding ways to persuade others to hold him up. In order to persuade others to let him cling to them Clinging Vine must appear very good or very deserving or both. Because he is a "good" person, the innocent victim of a sad fate beyond his control, he "deserves" the support of others; moreover, if they don't let him cling to them they are bad people. An accomplished Clinging Vine is skilled at making others feel guilty if they don't do what he wants them to do. Of course, the more egocentric other people are, and therefore subject to false guilt, the more likely they are to fall prey to Clinging Vine's tricks. Eventually, however, people get tired of holding Clinging Vine up; they get exasperated and withdraw their help. This leads to the ego crisis that Clinging Vine fears; it seems like the dreadful abyss, the worst thing that could happen. It is in fact the moment when he just might find what really holds him up; then he can give up his need to cling to others.

The Star wants admiration. She wants to be on the center of the stage, the admired and glorified person. In order to gain admirers she must find something she can do that will merit adulation. Perhaps she will get all A's in school, or be a great athlete, or collect boy friends by the dozen, or become a perfect parent. If she lacks talent, and all else fails, she can star at being "good," for almost anyone can pose as a "good" person if one tries hard enough. As long as Star is the admired person she feels secure, but if one day she shouldn't be admired, then the ego crisis comes. Maybe one day she gets a "C" instead of all "A's," or her boy friends desert her, or her children turn out badly, or her shadow gets in the way and the good little girl does something awful, or, God forbid, maybe a more accomplished Star gets on the stage with her and she is forgotten. This creates − 100, a dreadful, dark state which, however, can lead her to her true Self if she consents to go through the darkness even though it seems like death.

Turtle believes life is overwhelming. She thinks she can't cope with a world that is so frightening and therefore finds ways to hide from it. Sometimes Turtle is overwhelmed by everything; then she may find the ultimate security of the back ward of a hospital. Sometimes it is one particular area where she is a Turtle. For instance, she may be afraid to feel anything because her feelings are so painful, so she fashions a hard shell around herself and lives inside of this where she can feel safe. Turtles try to escape from life's dangers because they are afraid, and they are afraid because life is always trying to drag them out of their shells. A Turtle can escape from lots of things but never from the Self, which is right there with her inside of her shell but appears now as a dreadful enemy. Sooner or later something comes along that is especially hard to avoid. Then the Turtle will try all her tricks to get back into a safe place. If she succeeds her life will be more impoverished than ever, but if she can't succeed, and finally goes out to meet the threat, she can go through the ego crisis that will strip away her egocentricity and she can enter into a creative life.

Nero (Tyrant) protects himself by controlling others. His goal is always to be in the dominant position. Then he feels secure, and realizes an egocentric satisfaction—though not without a nagging guilty conscience that leaves him paranoid about other people. For at the bottom, every Nero is afraid that one day people will not be controlled, that the people he is dominating may rebel against him. If this happens, he is on his own cross at last, and if he consents to the suffering this brings him he just may go through it to a resurrected and new life. What at first appears like the worst thing that could happen contains the seeds of his salvation if he can accept his vulnerable, tender feelings and give up his need to always be on top.

A few more points need to be mentioned. Although in describing the four types I have used the pronouns "he" to refer to the Clinging Vine and Nero, and "she" to refer to Star and Turtle, persons of either sex may belong to any of the four egocentric types.

We may also have more than one egocentric pattern. For instance, at his office a man may be a terrible Nero, dominating all his subordinates and making their lives miserable, but when he is home, where intimacy is called for, he may be a Turtle, hiding behind his newspaper and avoiding real relationships with his wife and children.

One egocentric pattern can also revert to another. For instance, if a Nero is defeated he readily reverts to a Turtle. That's why a bully turns craven when he is beaten. A Star similarly often becomes a Clinging Vine when she can no longer be center-stage.

No one is entirely egocentric. There is always an admixture in us of the Real Self and the egocentric ego. Sometimes we come from one position and sometimes from the other. When we say of someone, "Oh I know just what she'll say or just what she'll do," it may indicate that this person always comes from an egocentric posture, for egocentric attitudes and responses are rigid and don't change. But every now and then someone may fool us and produce an unexpected and creative response. A creative ego response to a difficult situation is always possible as long as the Real Self can come through.

Kunkel's ideas about egocentricity apply to nations as well as individuals because the inhabitants of a nation identify with their collective situation in such a way as to create a national ego. The Soviet Union, for instance, seems to partake of the qualities of both Turtle and Nero. Outwardly there is the Nero attitude of brutal dominance, but inwardly is paranoid Turtle afraid of what appears to be a dangerous and threatening world. The United States seems to partake of both Star and Nero qualities.

There is much more we could say about Jung and Kunkel. In these few pages we have only begun to scratch the surface of their thoughts, but we have said enough to be able to study the life of Saul with the helpful insights of depth psychology.

Appendix B
The Alternate Version
of Saul's Rejection

As we have seen, there are frequently two or more versions of the same incident in the biblical story of Saul, and it often makes little difference which version we follow. However, in the case of Saul's purported disobedience to Yahweh there are two accounts that are markedly different from each other. I chose one and ignored the other, and an explanation for this is called for since one account favors Saul and the other shows him in a bad light.

The account I did not mention, which I will call the second version to distinguish it from the first story of Saul on Mount Gilgal, is found in 1 Samuel 15. In this story, Saul is told by Samuel that Yahweh wants him to wage war against the Amalekites, and that they are to be put "under the ban." This meant that every living thing was to be destroyed, including all the Amalekites' domestic animals and the Amalekite King Agag himself. Saul, however, does not kill all the sheep and oxen but spares the best of them, and does not execute King Agag. When Samuel catches Saul in this disobedience he tells him that Yahweh has rejected him and chosen another person to take his place as king. Saul offers excuses for his actions, but they are unconvincing and Samuel passes unrelenting judgment upon him.

As with all of the alternate accounts of the same incident that we find in the Saul saga, there is no way to establish definitively which, if either, version is most historically reliable. With this in mind I obviously chose the version that best suited my argument. If an attorney for the defense, which is what I have fancied myself to be for Saul, discovers two witnesses for the prosecution who have different testimony regarding the key issue, he will naturally concentrate on that witness who shows his client in the best light.

There is another reason, however, for my choice of the first version over the second: in the first version there is evidence that the unconscious is speaking. While I was able to use the first version to defend Saul and put Samuel in a bad light there is no reason to believe that this was the intention of the originators of this story. The persons who told both version one and version two agreed that Saul was to blame and that Samuel was justified in his condemnation of Saul. What happened in version one was that the raconteur "slipped" and allowed into his story evidence to the contrary. To put it another way, tradition universally agreed, and still does, that Saul was the "bad guy" and Samuel blameless, but in one account a repressed point of view, namely that Samuel was responsible for the trouble, crept in anyway. It is in just this way that the unconscious brings out the truth of a situation by correcting an erroneous conscious attitude. For this reason, I believe that the unconscious, so to speak, is on my side.

Index

129, 130, 133; anima, 58; as Center, 127, 128; creative, 78, 128; dark side of, 58, 59; defined, 122; and ego, 79, 122–127, 130, 132; evil, 78; and God/Yahweh, 56, 124; individuation, 126; Kunkel, 78, 127; psyche, 57; Real, 15, 28, 30, 31, 33, 44, 50, 62, 77, 103, 129, 134, 135; relationship, 75; royal, 31, 92; vessel of divine grace, 124; "we", 31, 127

shadow: 14, 16, 30, 35, 56, 124, 125, 133; defined, 124; Samuel's, 17

Shakespeare: 105, 110; *Hamlet*, 5

shaman(s): 23, 24, 65

Sharp, Daryl: 129

Sheol: 101, 109, 111

Shining Sands: 23

sin(s): 43, 55, 79, 127; Saul's, 4; Parsifal's, 53

soul(s): 49, 52, 55, 56, 65, 67, 71, 78, 79, 89, 96, 98, 99, 106, 113, 115; cure of, 4

sour grapes: 14

spirit(s): 5, 31, 32, 58, 92, 107, 109, 130; dark, 52; evil, 51, 55, 56, 58; from God, 61, 62, 64, 70; religious, 7; of Yahweh, 29–31, 51, 55, 60, 76

Star: 68, 74, 75, 84, 85, 87, 132–135

Story of the Bible—Hurlbut: 5

storyteller(s): 3, 4, 65, 110; Royalist tradition, 4; Anti-Royalist, 4

success(es): 2, 39, 51–54, 69, 75, 76

suffering: 63, 80, 96, 134

suicide: 117, 118; the oriental ethic, 118

symbol(s): 40; of the unconscious 125; of the Self, 124

Symbolic Quest, The—Whitmont: 124fn

Tao: 24

Tolstoy: 11

truth: 5, 6, 15, 40, 85, 89, 90, 108, 114, 137; ego crisis, 131

Turtle: 27, 28, 50, 75, 112, 132–135; Self, 133

unconscious, the: 16, 18, 19, 49, 51, 54, 56, 61, 87, 97, 107–109, 124, 125, 137; active imagination, 72; collective, 56, 110, 125; ego, 122; images of, 56, 81; Self, 122; source of energy, 130; symbols, 125

unconsciousness: 14, 50, 92

Urim and Thummim: 24

van der Post, Laurens: 88

vessel: 123, 124

Walaskay, Paul W.: 66

Whitmont, Edward: 124fn

what we don't know: 15–16